# SIX LITTLE BUNKERS
# AT UNCLE FRED'S

## LAURA LEE HOPE

1st WORLD
LIBRARY
Literary Society

# Six Little Bunkers at Uncle Fred's

Laura Lee Hope

© 1st World Library, 2007
PO Box 2211
Fairfield, IA 52556
www.1stworldlibrary.com
First Edition

LCCN: 2007930816

Softcover ISBN: 978-1-4218-4849-5
Hardcover ISBN: 978-1-4218-4752-8
eBook ISBN: 978-1-4218-4946-1

Purchase *"Six Little Bunkers at Uncle Fred's"*
as a traditional bound book at:
www.1stWorldLibrary.com/purchase.asp?ISBN=978-1-4218-4849-5

1st World Library is a literary, educational organization
dedicated to:

- Creating a free internet library of downloadable ebooks

- Hosting writing competitions and offering book publishing scholarships.

Interested in more 1st World Library books? contact:
literacy@1stworldlibrary.com
Check us out at: www.1stworldlibrary.com

# 1<sup>st</sup> World Library Literary Society

## Giving Back to the World

"If you want to work on the core problem, it's early school literacy."

**- James Barksdale, former CEO of Netscape**

"No skill is more crucial to the future of a child, or to a democratic and prosperous society, than literacy."

**- Los Angeles Times**

"Literacy... means far more than learning how to read and write... The aim is to transmit... knowledge and promote social participation."

**- UNESCO**

"Literacy is not a luxury, it is a right and a responsibility. If our world is to meet the challenges of the twenty-first century we must harness the energy and creativity of all our citizens."

**- President Bill Clinton**

"Parents should be encouraged to read to their children, and teachers should be equipped with all available techniques for teaching literacy, so the varying needs and capacities of individual kids can be taken into account."

**- Hugh Mackay**

# CONTENTS

# CHAPTER I

## A STRANGE RESCUE

"Can't I have a ride now, Russ? You said it would be my turn after Mun Bun."

"Yes, but, Margy, I haven't had enough ride yet!" declared Mun Bun.

"But when can I get in and have my ride?"

The three little children, two girls and a boy, stood in front of their older brother, Russ, watching him tying an old roller skate on the end of a board.

"Can't I have any more rides?" asked the smallest boy.

"In a minute, Mun Bun. As soon as I get this skate fastened on," answered Russ. "You rode so hard last time that you busted the scooter, and I've got to fix it. You broke the skate off!"

"I didn't mean to," and Mun Bun, who was called that because no one ever had the time to call him by his whole name, Munroe Ford Bunker—Mun Bun looked sorry for what had happened.

"I know you didn't," answered Russ.

"I didn't break anything, did I, Russ?" asked a little girl, with dark, curling hair and dark eyes, as she leaned over in front of her older brother, the better to see what he was doing. "I rided nice, didn't I, and I didn't break anything?"

"No, Margy, you didn't break anything," answered Russ. "And I'll give you a ride on the scooter pretty soon. Just wait till I get it fixed."

"And I want a ride, too!" exclaimed another girl, with curly hair of light color, and gray eyes that opened very wide. "Don't I get a ride, Russ? And what makes the wheels make such a funny sound when they go 'round? And what makes you call it a scooter? And can you make it go backwards? And—"

"Oh, I can't answer all those questions, Vi!" exclaimed Russ. "You're always asking questions, Daddy says. You wait and I'll give you a ride."

The four Bunker children—there were six of them, and you will meet the other two soon. The four Bunker children were playing up in the attic of their home. The attic was not as large as the attic of Grandpa Ford's house on Great Hedge Estate nor were there so many nice things in it. But still it did very well on a rainy afternoon, and Russ, Margy, Violet and Mun Bun were having a good time on the "scooter" Russ had made.

The way Russ made a "scooter" was this. He found a long board, one that the carpenters had left after they had made a storeroom for Mrs. Bunker in the attic, and to the board he fastened, on each end, part of an old roller skate. This gave the scooter two wheels on either end. The wheels were not

Laura Lee Hope

very large, nor very wide, and unless you sat right in the middle of the board of the scooter you might get tipped over. This had happened several times, and when Mun Bun was on, having a ride, he not only tipped over, but he ran into a trunk that stood in the attic, and knocked off one of the skates.

"Now I have to tie it on again!" Russ had exclaimed, and this had caused a stop in the fun.

"Can you fix it?" asked Margy, as she watched her brother. She wanted another ride, for the one she had had was a short one. Mun Bun was the youngest of the six little Bunkers, and they generally let him have more turns than any one else.

"Oh, yes, I can fix it," said Russ, who now began to whistle. And when Russ whistled, when he was making anything, you could generally tell that everything was coming out right.

Russ very often made things, but he did not always whistle over them. Often the things he made were such a puzzle that he could not think how to make them come out right and also think of a whistle-tune at the same time. But now he was all right, and so he whistled merrily as he put more string on the roller skate that he was fastening to the board of the scooter.

"Is it almost done?" asked Mun Bun, leaning over eagerly.

"Almost," answered Russ. "I want to look at the back wheels to see if they're all right, and then you can have a ride."

Russ gave the string a last turn, tied several knots in it, and then turned the board around. As he did so Margy uttered a cry.

"Ouch!" she exclaimed.

"What's the matter?" asked Russ.

"You banged me with the scooter," answered the little girl.

"Oh, I didn't mean to," said Russ. "I'm sorry! You can have an extra ride for that." Russ was very kind to his little brothers and sisters.

"It doesn't hurt very much," said Margy, rubbing the elbow that had been hit when Russ swung the board around.

Russ now bent over the other wheels on the end of the scooter. He found them a bit loose, as string will stretch and really isn't very good with which to fasten wheels on. But it was the best Russ could do.

Outside an early spring rain beat against the windows of the attic. It was cold outside, too, for the last winter snow had, only a week before, melted from the ground, which was still frozen in places. But it was nice and warm up in the attic, and there the Bunker children were having a fine time. The attic, as I have said, was not as big as Grandpa Ford's, but the children were having a good time, and even a smaller attic would have answered as well in the rain.

"Now I guess it's all ready for more rides," said Russ, as he put the scooter down on the floor.

"I'm going to get on!" cried Mun Bun.

"Wait until I put it straight," called Russ. "Then you can have a longer ride."

He took the board, with the roller skate wheels on either end, to a far corner of the attic. From there it could be pushed all the way across to the other wall.

Just as Mun Bun was about to take his place, so that Russ could push him across the attic floor, footsteps were heard coming up the stairs that led to the third story of the Bunker house.

Then a boy's voice called:

"What are you doing?"

"Riding on a scooter Russ made," answered Violet. "Oh, it's lots of fun! Come on, Laddie!"

Laddie was Violet's twin brother, and he had the same kind of curly hair and gray eyes as had his sister.

"Did you make that?" asked Laddie of Russ.

"Sure."

"Will it hold me?"

"Sure. It'll hold me. I had a ride on it."

"Say, that's great!" cried Laddie. "We can have lots of fun on that! I'm glad I came up."

"Well, come all the way up, and stand out of the way!" ordered Russ. "The train's going to start. Toot! Toot! All aboard!"

Laddie hurried up the last few steps and took his place in a corner, out of the way of the scooter with Mun Bun on it. A girl with light, fluffy hair, and bright, smiling eyes, followed him. She was a year younger than Russ, who was eight years old.

"Oh, Rose!" cried Violet, as she saw her older sister. "We're having such fun!"

"You can have a ride, too, Rose! Can't she?" asked Mun Bun of Russ. "Go on, push me!"

"Yes, we'll all take turns having rides," said Russ. "If I could find another roller skate I'd make another scooter, and then we could have races."

"If we had two we could make believe they were two trains, and have 'em bump into each other and have collisions and all that!" cried Laddie. "That'll be fun! Come on, let's do it!"

"We'll have to get another board and another skate," said Russ. "We'll look after a while. Now I'm going to give Mun Bun a ride."

He shoved the scooter across the floor of the attic. Mun Bun kept tight hold with his chubby hands of the edges of the board, in the middle of which he sat, between the two pieces of roller skate that made wheels for the scooter.

"Hi! Yi!" yelled Mun Bun. "This is fun!"

"Now it's my turn!" exclaimed Margy. "Get off, Mun Bun."

"I have to have a ride back! I've got to have a ride back!" he cried. "Russ said he'd ride me across the attic and back again! Didn't you, Russ?"

"Yes, that's what I did. Well, here we go back."

Laura Lee Hope

He had pushed Mun Bun to the far side of the attic, and was pushing the little fellow back again, when Laddie cried:

"Oh, I know a better way than that."

"For what?" asked Russ.

"For having rides," went on Laddie. "We can make a hill and let the scooter slide downhill. Then you won't have to push anybody."

"How can you make a hill?" asked Russ.

"Out of mother's ironing-board," was the answer. "It's down in the kitchen. I'll get it. Don't you know how we used to put it up on a chair and then slide down on the ironing-board?"

"Oh, I remember!" cried Rose.

"Then we can do that," went on Laddie. "It'll be packs of fun!"

"Well, you get the ironing-board," said Russ.

"I'll help," offered Violet. "I'll help you get the board, Laddie."

"All right, come on," he called, and the two children started down the attic stairs.

While he was waiting for them to come back Russ gave Margy and Rose each a ride on the scooter. It really went very well over the smooth floor of the attic, for the roller-skate wheels turned very easily, even if they did get crooked now and then because the strings with which they were tied on, slipped.

Up the stairs, bumpity bump, came Laddie and Vi with the ironing-board.

"Mother wasn't there, and I didn't see Norah, so I just took the board," said Laddie. "Now we'll put one end on a box and the other end on the floor, and we'll have a hill. Then we can ride the scooter downhill just like we rode our sleds at Grandpa Ford's."

"Yes, I guess we can," said Russ.

There were several boxes in the attic, and some of these were dragged to one end. On them one end of the ironing-board was raised, so that it sloped down like a hill. Of course it was not a very big one, but then the Bunkers were not very large children, nor was the scooter Russ had made very long. By squeezing them on, it would hold two children.

"Who's going down first?" asked Russ, as he and Laddie fixed the ironing-board hill in place, and wheeled the scooter over to it.

"I will!" exclaimed Mun Bun. "I like to ride."

"You'd better let us try first," said Laddie. "It might go so fast it would knock into something."

"I'll go down!" decided Russ. "It's my scooter, because I made it; and so I'll go down first."

"But I made the hill!" objected Laddie. "It's my hill."

"Then why don't both of you go down together?" asked Rose. "If it will hold you two boys it will be all right for us girls. You go three times, then Vi and I will take three turns."

"All right—that's what we will," said Russ. "Come on, Laddie."

Some boxes had been piled back of the one on which the ironing-board rested in a slanting position, and these boxes made a level place on which to get a start. Russ and Laddie lifted the scooter up there, and got up themselves. Then they carefully sat down on the board to which were fastened the roller-skate wheels.

"All ready?" asked Russ, who was in front, holding to a rope, like a sled rope, by which he hoped to guide the scooter. "All ready, Laddie?"

"All ready," was the answer.

"Here we go!" cried Russ.

He gave a little shove with his feet, and down the ironing-board hill ran the scooter, carrying Russ and Laddie with it. The first time it ran beautifully.

"This is great!" cried Laddie.

"Fine!" exclaimed his brother.

And then, all of a sudden, something happened. The scooter ran off the hill sideways, and started over the attic floor toward Rose, Vi, Mun Bun and Margy. They squealed and screamed and tried to get out of the way. But Mun Bun fell down, and Margy fell over him, and Vi fell over Margy, and Rose fell over Violet. So there the four little Bunkers were, all in a heap, and the scooter, with Russ and Laddie on it, running toward the brother and sisters.

"Stop! Stop it!" cried Laddie.

"I can't!" shouted Russ, pulling on the guide rope. But that did no good.

"Oh, we're going to knock into 'em!" yelled Laddie.

And right into the other children ran the scooter. Russ and Laddie were thrown off, and, for a moment, there was a bumping, thumping, yelling, crying and screaming noise.

Mun Bun, trying to roll out of the way, knocked a box down off a trunk, and the box had some croquet balls in it, which rumbled over the attic floor almost like thunder.

In the midst of all this noise and confusion some one came running up the stairs. A man entered the attic, and took one look at the mass of struggling children on the floor.

"My good land!" he cried. "I wonder if I can save any of 'em! Oh, what a mix-up!"

Then the stranger started in to rescue the six little Bunkers, for they were all tangled up.

Laura Lee Hope

# CHAPTER II

## UNCLE FRED

"Are you hurt? Are any of you hurt? What happened, anyhow? Did part of the house fall on you?"

The man who had run up the attic stairs went on picking up first one and then another of the six little Bunkers. For a time they were so excited over what had happened that they paid no attention to him.

But when the stranger picked Rose up and set her on her feet, the little girl took a good look at him, and, seeing a strange man in the attic, she cried:

"Oh, it's a burglar! It's a burglar! Oh, Mother! Norah! Jerry Simms! It's a burglar!"

"Hush, child! Don't shout like that or you'll have all the neighbors in!" said the man. "Be quiet, and I'll tell you who I am! Don't yell any more!"

Rose stopped yelling, her mouth still wide open, ready for another shout, and looked at the man. He smiled at her and picked up Mun Bun out from under the box from which the croquet balls had fallen.

"Who is you?" asked Mun Bun.

"I'll tell you in just a moment, if you don't make such a racket," said the stranger, smiling kindly.

The six little Bunkers became quiet at once, but before I tell you who the strange man is I want to say just a few words about the children in this story, and relate to you something about the other books in this series.

To begin at the beginning, there were six little Bunkers, as I have told you. There was Russ, aged eight, a great whistler and a boy very fond of making toys, such as scooters and other things.

Next to him was Rose, a year younger.

Then came Violet and Laddie. They both had curly hair and gray eyes, and were six years old each, which makes twelve in all, you see. They were twins, and each one had a funny habit. Vi asked a great many questions, some of which could be answered, some of which could not be answered, and to some of which she didn't wait for an answer.

Laddie was very fond of asking queer little riddles. Some were good, and it took quite a while to think of the answer he wanted. Others didn't seem to have any answer. And some were not really riddles at all. But he had fun asking them.

Next in order was Margy, whose real name was Margaret, just as Laddie's real name was Fillmore Bunker. But he was seldom called that. Margy was aged five. She had dark hair and eyes.

Then there was Mun Bun, or Munroe Ford Bunker, her little brother, who was four years old, and had blue eyes and golden hair.

Now you have met the six little Bunkers. Of course there was Daddy Bunker, whose name was Charles. He was in the real estate business in Pineville, Pennsylvania, and his office was almost a mile from his home, on the main street. Mother Bunker's name was Amy, and before her marriage she had been Miss Amy Bell.

Besides this there were in the Bunker family two others: Norah O'Grady, the cook, and Jerry Simms, an old soldier, who could tell fine stories of the time he was in the army. Now Jerry ran the Bunker automobile, cut the grass, sprinkled the lawn and attended to the furnace in winter.

But the Bunker family had relatives, and it was on visits to some of these that the children had had many adventures. First you may read "Six Little Bunkers at Grandma Bell's." This is the book that begins the series, and tells of the visit the family made at Grandma Bell's at Lake Sagatook in Maine. There they found an old lumberman and he had some papers which Daddy Bunker wanted to get back. And, oh, yes! Grandma Bell was Mrs. Bunker's mother.

After that the children went to visit their father's sister in Boston, and the book which tells all about that, and the strange pocketbook Rose found, is called "Six Little Bunkers at Aunt Jo's."

On leaving Aunt Jo's the family paid a visit to another relative. This was Mr. Thomas Bunker, who was the son of Mr. Ralph Bunker, and Ralph was Daddy Bunker's brother, who had died.

In "Six Little Bunkers at Cousin Tom's" I told you the story of the fun the children had at the seashore, and how a gold locket was lost and strangely found again.

The book just before this one is called "Six Little Bunkers at Grandpa Ford's," and there was quite a mystery about a ghost at Great Hedge Estate, in New York State, where Mr. Ford lived.

Grandpa Ford was Daddy Bunker's step-father, but no real father could have been more kind, nor have loved the six little Bunkers any more than he did. The children spent the winter at Great Hedge Estate, and helped find out what made the queer noises. And if you want to find out I suggest that you read the book.

Christmas and New Year's had been celebrated at Grandpa Ford's, and when winter was about to break up the Bunkers had come back home to Pineville. Daddy Bunker said he needed to look after the spring real estate business, for that was the best time of the year for selling and buying houses and lots, and renting places.

So they said good-bye to Grandpa Ford, and took the train back home. The six little Bunkers had been in their own house about a month now, and they were playing in the attic, as I have told you, with the scooter Russ had made, when the accident happened.

Then, as I have told you, up the attic stairs rushed a strange man, who pulled Mun Bun out of the tangle of arms and legs. And Rose thought the strange man was a burglar.

"But I'm not," he said, smiling at the children. "Don't you know who I am?"

Russ shook his head.

"How did you get in here?" asked Violet. As usual, she was first with a question.

"I just walked in," said the man in answer. "I was coming here anyhow, and when I got here I saw the door wide open, so I just walked in."

"Did you come to sell something?" asked Rose. "'Cause if you did I don't believe my mother wants anything. She's got everything she wants."

"Well, she's got a nice lot of children, anyhow," said the man, smiling on each and ever one of the six little Bunkers in turn. "I'll say that. She has a nice lot of children, and I'm very glad none of you is hurt.

"As I said, I was coming here anyhow, and when I got on the porch and saw the door open, I walked right in. Then I heard a terrible racket up here in the attic, and up I rushed. I thought maybe the house was falling down."

"No," said Russ as he pulled his scooter out from between two trunks, "it was this. We slid down the ironing-board hill, Laddie and I, and it went off crooked—the scooter did."

"And it knocked into us," said Violet. "But if you didn't come to sell anything, what did you come for?"

"Well," said the strange man, and he smiled again, "you might say I came to get you children."

"You—you came to get *us*?" gasped Rose.

"Yes. I'm going to take you away with me."

"Take—take us *away* with you!" cried Russ. "We won't go! We want to stay with our daddy and mother."

"I'll take them, too," said the man. "I have room for all you six little Bunkers and more too, out on my ranch. I've come to take you all away with me."

What could it mean? Russ and Rose, the oldest, could not understand it. They looked at the man again. They were sure they had never seen him before.

"Yes," the stranger went on, "I saw the door open, so I walked in. I was glad to get out of the rain. It's a cold storm. I hope summer will soon come. And, as I say, I've come to take you away."

If the man had not smiled so nicely the children might have been frightened. But, as it was, they knew everything would be all right.

"And now, as long as none of you is hurt, I think I'd better go downstairs and tell your mother I have come to take you away," went on the man. "I think I hear her coming up."

And, just then, footsteps were heard on the stairs leading to the attic, and Mrs. Bunker appeared.

"Oh, Mother," gasped out Rose, "there's a man here and he says he's going to take us away and—"

Before she finished Mrs. Bunker had run up to the attic. She looked at the strange man, who smiled at her. Then she hurried over to him and kissed him and said:

"Oh, Fred, I'm glad to see you! I didn't expect you until to-morrow, and I was going to surprise the children with you.

Laura Lee Hope

Oh, but I'm glad to see you! Children," she said, laughing, "this is my brother, your Uncle Fred."

# CHAPTER III

## A QUEER STORY

The six little Bunkers, who had been untangled from the mix-up caused when the scooter ran sideways off the ironing-board hill, stood in a half circle and looked at the strange man. He did not seem quite so strange now, and he certainly smiled in a way the children liked.

"Is he our real uncle?" asked Violet.

"Yes, he is your very own uncle. He is my brother. Frederic is his name—Frederic Bell," went on Mother Bunker. "But you are to call him Uncle Fred."

"Then he *isn't* a burglar!" stated Rose.

"Of course not!" laughed her mother.

"No, I'm not a burglar," said the visitor, laughing too. "Though I don't blame you for feeling a bit alarmed when I rushed in. I thought some of you might know me, though some of you I've never seen, and Russ and Rose were smaller than they are now the last time I saw them."

"I didn't tell them you were coming," said Mrs. Bunker. "I

hardly thought you would get here so soon, and I was planning a surprise, as I say. But we're very glad to see you. How did you get into the house and up here?"

"I walked in. The front door was open and—"

"I left it open to air the house."

"And as soon as I got in I heard a great racket up where I knew the attic must be, so up I rushed. I found the children all in a heap, and I pulled them apart as best I could."

"We were riding on a scooter I made from an older roller skate," explained Russ, "and it went off the ironing-board sideways and it bumped into everybody."

"I should say it did bump!" laughed Uncle Fred.

"But we're not hurt," added Laddie. "We're all right now. Can you answer riddles, Uncle Fred?"

"Well, yes, I think so, if they're not too hard."

"I know lots of riddles," said Laddie. "I have a good one about what goes through—"

"Wait a minute!" cried Vi, elbowing her way to a place in the front ranks of the six little Bunkers. "I want to ask Uncle Fred a question."

"You did ask him one," suggested Rose.

"Well, I want to ask him another," went on Vi. "You said you were going to take us away," she told the visitor. "Are you? And where and when are we all going? And can we have some fun?"

"Oh, hold on! Stop! Whoa! Back up!" exclaimed Uncle Fred. "I thought you said you wanted to ask *one* question, not half a dozen."

"But you said you were going to take us away. Are you?"

"I am if your mother and father will let me," replied Uncle Fred. "You know I wrote you," he went on to Mother Bunker, "that I'd like to have you all come out to my ranch to stay all summer."

"What's a ranch?" asked Vi.

"I know," interrupted Russ. "It's a place where they have horses and cows and—"

"Indians!" cried Laddie.

"And cowboys!" went on Russ. "That'll be great! We can have a Wild West show!"

"Oh, let's go!" shouted Laddie.

"Children! Children!" murmured Mother Bunker. "Less noise, please! What will Uncle Fred think of you?"

"Oh, I don't mind the noise," replied the Westerner. "I'm used to that. Sometimes, when the cowboys are feeling pretty good, they whoop and yell like Indians."

"Are there any Indians out there?" asked Russ eagerly. "I mean out at your ranch?"

"Yes, a few," answered Uncle Fred.

"And where is your ranch?" Laddie inquired.

All interest in the scooter was lost in Uncle Fred's arrival. And if he planned to take the six little Bunkers somewhere they wanted to hear all about that. So they crowded close around him.

"My ranch," said Uncle Fred, "is out in Montana, near a place called Moon City. The name of my place is Three Star, and—"

"Is there a moon, too?" asked Violet.

"Well, the name of the town, as I said, is Moon City, and I suppose it was named that because the moon looks so beautiful over the mountains. But I am down on the plains, and the reason I call my ranch Three Star is because my cattle are marked with three stars, so I will know them if they should happen to get mixed up with the cattle of another ranch."

"When are we going?" asked Russ. "I have to make a lasso if we go out on a ranch. Maybe I'll lasso an Indian."

"So'll I," put in Laddie. "When can we go, Mother?"

"Oh, not for some little time. Uncle Fred has come to pay us a visit. Haven't you?" she went on to her brother.

"Oh, yes, I'm going to stay East a while," he said. "But I'm desirous of getting back to Three Star," he added. "There's something queer been going on there, and I want to find out what it is. That's one reason I came on East—to try to find out what's wrong at my place. There certainly is something queer there!"

"Is it a ghost?" asked Violet.

"No, hardly a ghost," answered Uncle Fred with a laugh. "What do you know about ghosts, anyhow?"

"There was one at Grandpa Ford's," explained Rose.

"But we found out what it was," added Russ.

"But first it made terribly queer noises," said Laddie.

"Well, the only queer noises out at Three Star Ranch are made by the cowboys, and sometimes by the Indians," said Uncle Fred. "No, this is something different. But it might almost as well be a ghost for all I can find out about it. It certainly is very queer," he went on to his sister. "I have lost a great many cattle lately, and that and something strange about a spring of water on my place, are two of the reasons why I came on here. I want to talk with some men who know about springs and streams of water, and get some books about it so I can solve this puzzle, if it's possible.

"Another reason I came on," he added, "is to take you all back with me to Moon City, and let the children have fun out on my ranch."

"Do you mean to take us all out West?" asked Rose.

"Yes, every one of you six little Bunkers, and your father and mother, too," returned Uncle Fred.

"Can we go, Mother?" begged Russ.

"I'll see about it," was the answer. "But we'd all better go downstairs now. Uncle Fred must be tired from his long trip, and I want to get him a cup of tea. It is raining hard still, so you children can't go out and play."

"We don't want to," said Vi. "We want to see Uncle Fred."

"I like Uncle Fred!" exclaimed Mun Bun, going up to his mother's brother and clasping his hand. "I like him awful much!"

"And I like you, too," replied Uncle Fred, catching the little fellow up in his arms.

"I like him, too!" exclaimed Margy, who was not going to be left out.

"That's the girl! I knew you wouldn't forget me!" and with a laugh Uncle Fred caught her up also, and danced about the attic, with a child in each arm.

"Is it far out to your ranch?" asked Russ.

"Quite a way, little man," answered Uncle Fred. "It will take us about four days to get there, riding steadily on the train. But we won't start right away. I have some business to do here. But when that is over I hope the weather will be better, and then we can start."

"And stay out there all summer?" asked Laddie.

"Yes, and all winter, too, if you like. We'll be glad to have you."

"We seem to do nothing but visit around of late!" exclaimed Mother Bunker. "We have been to Grandma Bell's, to Aunt Jo's, to Cousin Tom's, to Grandpa Ford's and now maybe we're going to Uncle Fred's."

"I think it's nice," remarked Rose.

"So do I!" added Vi. "I love to go visiting!"

"Could I ask you that riddle now?" inquired Laddie, as Uncle Fred started downstairs, carrying Margy and Mun Bun.

"Yes," was the answer of the children's uncle. "Go ahead."

"What is it that goes through—"

"Oh, don't ask him that one about what goes through a door but doesn't come into the room!" exclaimed Russ.

"I wasn't!" asserted Laddie. "That's an old one, and the answer is a keyhole. I was going to ask him a new one."

"Well, go ahead," said Uncle Fred.

"What is it goes through—No, that isn't it. Let me see. I almost forgot. Oh, I know! What can you drive without a whip or reins? That's it. What can you drive without a whip or reins?"

"Do you mean an ox?" asked Uncle Fred. "I've seen oxen driven, and the man who drove them didn't use reins as they do on horses, though he did have a goad, which is like a whip."

"No, oxen isn't the answer," said Laddie. "Do you give up?"

"Well, I will, just to see what the answer is," replied Uncle Fred.

"What is it you can drive without a whip or reins?" asked Laddie again. "The answer is a nail. You can drive that with a hammer."

"Ha! Ha! That's a pretty good riddle!" laughed Uncle Fred. "I must try that on some of the cowboys when I get back to Three Star Ranch."

"And now don't you children bother Uncle Fred too much while I'm making him a cup of tea," said Mrs. Bunker, as they reached the first floor.

"Oh, they don't bother me," declared Uncle Fred.

"Tell us about the something queer on your ranch," begged Russ, as his uncle sat down, holding Margy and Mun Bun in his lap.

"All right, I will," promised Mr. Bell. "First I'll tell you about the ranch, and then about the queer things that happened. Now Three Star Ranch is—"

Just then the doorbell rang loudly, and Uncle Fred stopped speaking.

"I wonder who it is," said Rose.

# CHAPTER IV

## UNCLE FRED'S TALE

The ringing of the Bunker doorbell was not unusual. It often rang during the day, but just now, when Uncle Fred was about to tell his story, it rather surprised the children to hear the tinkle.

"I'll go and see who it is," offered Russ. "And please don't tell any of the story until I come back," he begged.

"I won't," promised Uncle Fred.

Russ hurried to the door, and, as he opened it, the other children heard him cry:

"Oh, Daddy! What made you ring?"

"I forgot my key," answered Mr. Bunker. "I couldn't open the door."

"Oh, it's Daddy!" cried Mun Bun and Margy, and, slipping down from Uncle Fred's knee, they raced to the hall to get their usual kisses.

"Guess who's here!" cried Russ, for his father could not see into the room where his wife's brother sat. "Guess!"

"Grandma Bell?"

"Nope!"

"Aunt Jo?"

"Nope!"

"It's Uncle Fred!" cried Rose, hurrying out into the hall. "And he's got a secret out at his ranch like Grandpa Ford had at Great Hedge, and he's going to take us all out there and—and—"

"My! better stop and catch your breath before it runs away from you," laughed Daddy Bunker, as he lifted Rose in his arms and kissed her. "So Uncle Fred is here, is he? He came a little ahead of time."

"And he s'prised us all up in the attic," added Laddie, who had also come into the hall. "Russ and I rode down on the scooter, and we bumped, and had a mix-up, and Uncle Fred came up, and—"

"And we thought he was a burglar!" finished Violet.

"You must have had quite a time," laughed Daddy Bunker. "Well, now, after I get my wet things off, I'll go in and see Uncle Fred and hear all about it," and soon Daddy Bunker and his wife's brother were shaking hands and talking, while the children sat about them, eager and listening.

"We'll have an early supper," said Mother Bunker, when she had given Uncle Fred a cup of tea, "and then we can hear all about Three Star Ranch."

Norah O'Grady soon had a nice supper on the table, and after Rose had helped with it, as she often did, for her mother was teaching her little daughter to be a housekeeper, the children took their places and began to eat. And, at the same time, they listened to the talk that went on among the grown folk. Mother and Father Bunker had many questions to ask Uncle Fred, and he also asked them a great many, for he wanted to know all about Grandma Bell, and Aunt Jo and Grandpa Ford and all the rest of the Bunkers' relatives.

"And now will you tell us about Three Star Ranch?" asked Russ eagerly, as the chairs were pushed back.

"Yes, I will," promised Uncle Fred.

"And don't leave out the Indians," begged Laddie.

"Nor the cowboys," added Russ.

"Can you tell about some ponies?" asked Rose. "I love ponies!"

"Yes, I'll tell about them, too," said her uncle. "And if you come out West with me you shall have some rides on ponies."

"Really, truly?" gasped Rose.

"Oh, won't that be fun!" cried Vi. "What color are ponies? And what makes them be called ponies? I should think they would be called pawnies, 'cause they paw the ground. And how many have you, Uncle Fred?"

"Oh, Vi! Not so many questions, my dear! Please!" exclaimed her mother, laughing. "Uncle Fred won't get a chance to tell any story if you talk so much. You are a regular chatterbox to-night."

"Wait until you get out West. It's so big there you can talk all day and night and bother no one," said Uncle Fred. "But now I'll tell you about my ranch.

"As I mentioned, it is near Moon City, in Montana. That is a good many miles from here, and around my house are big fields, where the cattle roam about and eat the grass.

"A ranch, you must know, little Bunkers, is just a big farm. But instead of raising apples and peaches and pears, hay, grain or chickens on my ranch, I raise cattle. Cows you might call them, though we speak of them as cattle. Some men raise horses on their ranches, but though I have some horses and ponies, I have more cattle than anything else.

"I have to keep a number of men to look after the cattle. These men are called cowboys, and they ride about the ranch on horses, or cow ponies, and see that the cattle are all right, that they get enough to eat and drink, and that no one takes them away."

"What do the Indians do?" asked Russ. "Tell us about them."

"Well, some of the Indians farm," said Uncle Fred. "Some of them make baskets and other things to sell to travelers who come through on the trains, but many of them just live a lazy life. They are on what is called a Reservation—that is land which the government has set aside for them."

"Do Indians come to your ranch?" asked Laddie. "And could I lasso any of 'em with a rope lasso like I saw in some pictures?"

"Well, sometimes Indians do come to Three Star," answered

Uncle Fred. "But I don't believe any of them would like to be lassoed."

"What's this I hear about your having trouble?" asked Daddy Bunker.

"Well, yes, I have been having trouble," answered Uncle Fred. "And, as usual, my trouble is like that a lot of ranchers have. Some one has been taking my cattle."

"Didn't you want them to?" asked Russ.

"No, indeed," answered his uncle. "I raise my cattle to sell, so I can make money to pay my cowboys and live on some of it myself. If bad men take my cattle away in the night, as they do, without paying me, I lose money. And that's why I came on East here."

"Surely you didn't come all the way from Moon City to find out who was taking your cattle at Three Star Ranch!" exclaimed Mother Bunker.

"Oh, no. The men who are doing that are right out there. I've left some of my cowboys to attend to them," answered Uncle Fred. "What I came on for, besides getting you to go back with me, is to get some books about springs and streams of water, and also to talk with some engineers about a queer spring on my ranch."

"What sort of queer spring?" asked Daddy Bunker. "I thought all springs were alike."

"Well, I s'pose they are, in that they have water in 'em," said Uncle Fred. "But mine isn't that kind. Sometimes it has water in it, and again it hasn't."

"What do you mean?" asked his sister. "Does the spring go dry? That used to happen to the spring where we lived when we were children. Don't you remember, Fred?"

"Yes, but that spring only went dry when there was no rain— say in a dry, hot summer. The spring on Three Star Ranch goes dry sometimes in the middle of a rainy season."

"What makes it?" asked Daddy Bunker.

"That's what I came on to find out about," replied Uncle Fred. "None of my cowboys can tell what makes it, and the Indians are puzzled, too. It's like one of Laddie's riddles, I guess."

"That's what we thought about the ghost at Great Hedge," said Mrs. Bunker. "But we finally found out what it was, and very simple it was, too. Perhaps this spring of yours will turn out the same way."

"Well, I hope it does," said her brother. "All I know is that sometimes the spring will be full of fine water. We use it for drinking at the ranch house and for watering some of the horses. The cattle drink at a creek that runs through my place. That never goes dry.

"But sometimes there will be hardly a drop of water in the spring, and then there is trouble. Everybody is sorry then, for we have to haul water from the creek in barrels, and it isn't as good to drink as the spring water."

"Is that the only queer thing?" asked Daddy Bunker.

"No. The most remarkable thing about it," went on Uncle Fred, "is that every time the spring goes dry some of my cattle are taken away. I suppose you could call it stolen, though I don't like to think that any of my neighbors would steal. I used to think the cattle wandered away, but since none of them wander back again I feel pretty sure they must be taken on purpose."

"And every time the spring dries up the cattle are taken?" asked Mrs. Bunker, while the six little Bunkers listened eagerly to Uncle Fred's story.

"Almost every time. I don't know what causes it."

"Maybe the cows drink up all the water," said Russ.

"No, cattle don't come near the spring," said Mr. Bell. "They are on the far end of the ranch. It is a puzzle to me; about as much of a puzzle as the ghost must have been at Great Hedge, before you found out about it."

"So you came East to consult some engineers about the spring," remarked Daddy Bunker. "Do you think they can help you?"

"Well, you know there are engineers who make a study of all kinds of water; of springs, lakes, rivers, and so on," explained Uncle Fred. "They are water-engineers just as others are steam or electrical engineers. I thought I'd ask them the reasons for springs going dry. Some of them may know something about the water in Montana, and they can tell me if there are underground rivers or lakes that might do something to my spring.

"Anyhow I had some other business in New York, so while I was attending to that, and coming on here to get you folks, I thought I'd see the engineers."

"And have you seen any yet?" asked his sister.

"Not yet. I'm going to in a day or so. But I stopped at a store and ordered—"

Before Uncle Fred could say what it was he had ordered the doorbell rang again. This time it could not be Daddy Bunker coming in, as he was already at home.

Norah, who went to open the door, could be heard speaking to some one.

"Oh, and it's a message you have for Mr. Bell, is it?" she said. "Well, come in and don't be standin' there in the wet rain."

"A message for me!" exclaimed Uncle Fred. "I hope it isn't any bad news from my ranch—about more cattle being taken."

## CHAPTER V

## PACKING UP

"Somebody for you, Mr. Bell," announced Norah, as she opened wider the door of the sitting room where the six little Bunkers, Uncle Fred and the others were gathered. "It's a boy, and he has a package."

"Then it can't be a telegram containing bad news," said Uncle Fred. "They don't come in packages, unless there's a lot of 'em, and I hardly would get that many. I'll see what it is."

The boy was not a telegraph messenger after all, but a special delivery lad from the post-office, and the package he had for Uncle Fred was a book.

"Oh, it's a book I sent for to New York," said the ranchman after he had given the boy ten cents, and had opened the package.

"It's a book that tells about springs, and the rocks underneath the earth where the water comes from. I thought I'd read about springs so I'd learn something about the queer one on my ranch," Uncle Fred said to Daddy Bunker. "I heard about this book, sent to New York for it, and asked them to send it to me here by special delivery. Now I can read what I want to know about water."

"Will you read us a story out of the book?" asked Margy. "I like stories."

"I don't believe there are any stories in this book," said Uncle Fred with a laugh.

"Could you tell us one?" asked Mun Bun.

"About cowboys!" exclaimed Russ.

"And Indians!" added Laddie.

"Well, I guess I could think of a story, if I tried real hard," answered Uncle Fred, laughing.

The six little Bunkers gathered about his chair, and, laying aside the book that the special delivery messenger had brought, the ranchman told the children some wonderful stories.

He told them how, once, his cattle all ran away in a mad rush called a "stampede," and how he and his cowboys had to ride after them on ponies, firing their big revolvers, to turn the steers back from a deep gully.

"And did you stop 'em?" asked Russ, his eyes wide open in wonder and excitement.

"Oh, yes. But it was hard work," answered his uncle.

Then Mr. Bell told about a big prairie fire. On the flat, level fields, where he pastured his cattle, grew long grass. When this gets dry it burns very easily, and, once started, it is hard to stop.

"And how did you stop it?" asked Rose, when her uncle had told about the blazing miles of grass.

"We got a lot of men and horses and plows," he answered, "and plowed a wide strip of land in front of the fire. When the flames got to the bare ground there was nothing for them to burn, and the wind was not strong enough to carry them over to where there was more grass. So we saved our ranch houses."

"Do you live in a house on your ranch?" asked Laddie.

"Why, of course we do!" laughed Uncle Fred. "What did you think we lived in?"

"Tents, like the Indians."

"Oh, no, we have houses. But they aren't as nice as yours here in Pineville," said the ranchman. "I have a house to myself where I live with Captain Roy, and there is another house where the cowboys live. Then there is still another house where they eat their meals. This has a lot of big windows in it that can be opened wide on a hot day."

"Who is Captain Roy?" asked Russ. "Is he an old soldier, like Jerry Simms?"

"Yes, Captain Robert Roy used to be in the United States army," answered Uncle Fred. "He is retired now, and he helps me at the ranch. He is a partner of mine, and he looks after things while I am away. You six little Bunkers will like him, for he loves children."

"I wish we could hurry up and get out there!" sighed Russ.

"Well, I think the best place for my little chickens to hurry to is—*bed*!" laughed Mother Bunker. "Go to bed now, and morning will soon come, so we can talk about going to Uncle Fred's."

The children did not want to go to bed, but they always minded their mother, unless they forgot and did something she had told them not to. But this time there was no chance to forget.

"Good night, Uncle Fred!" they called, one after another, as they trooped upstairs.

Norah went with Mun Bun and Margy to see that they were properly undressed and covered up. Uncle Fred stayed downstairs to talk with Daddy and Mother Bunker.

He was telling them about the strange spring on his ranch, in which the water sometimes ran out in the night, no one knew where, and he was speaking about his cattle having been taken away, when suddenly Laddie called from upstairs:

"Mother, make Russ stop!"

"I'm not doing anything, Mother!" answered the voice of Russ, quickly enough.

"He is so!" went on Laddie. "He's playing he's a cowboy, and he says I've got to be an Indian, and he's going to lasso me with the sheet off the bed."

"Well, I didn't do it—not yet—did I?" asked Russ.

"No, but you're going to!"

"I am not!"

"You are so! You said you were."

"Well, I said I would if you'd let me."

"And I won't let you! I want to go to sleep so morning will come quick, and we can go to Uncle Fred's," went on Laddie. "I can think of some new riddles there."

"Boys! Boys! Be quiet and go to sleep!" called Mr. Bunker.

And, after a little more talk, Laddie and Russ settled down in bed and nothing more was heard of them until morning.

"Is Uncle Fred here?" eagerly asked Rose, when she came downstairs to breakfast.

"Of course he is," answered her mother. "What made you think he wasn't?"

"Oh, I—I dreamed in the night he went back home, and I couldn't see him any more," answered the little girl. "Did he go?"

"Indeed I didn't, Rose!" answered Uncle Fred himself, as he came softly up behind her and caught her up in his arms. "I'm going to stay here until you all get ready to go back to Three Star Ranch with me."

Then the rest of the little Bunkers came down, each one eager to see Uncle Fred and hear more of his wonderful stories of the West. And he was glad to tell them, for he liked the children, and, knowing they had never been out on a ranch, he realized how strange it all was to them.

"If we are really going West," said Mother Bunker to Daddy Bunker, after breakfast, "I must begin to think of packing up again. It seems we do nothing but travel!"

"The children like it," said her husband.

"Yes, and they'll like it out at my place," added Uncle Fred.

"Yes, I suppose so," said Mrs. Bunker. "But now to think of packing. It's such a long journey we can't take much."

"You won't need it," her brother said. "Though we live out West among the Indians and the cowboys, there are some stores there, and you can buy what you can't take with you. Besides, you won't need much for the children. Let them rough it. Put old clothes on them and let them roll around on the grass. That's the best thing in the world for them.

"Well, I'm going now to have a talk with some water engineers about my spring, and attend to some other business. Do you think you can be ready to go back with me in about a week?"

"Oh, never so soon as that!" cried Mrs. Bunker. "I'll need at least two weeks to pack up."

"All right, then we'll call it two weeks. So, two weeks from to-day, at ten o'clock in the morning," said Uncle Fred, "we start for the West."

"Hurray!" cried Russ, who came in just in time to hear what his uncle said.

The next two weeks were busy ones. The six little Bunkers could not do much toward packing, though Rose, who went about the house singing, as she almost always did, helped her mother as much as she could. Russ went about whistling, but he did not help much. Instead he and Laddie made lassos out of clotheslines, and once Mrs. Bunker heard Norah, out in the kitchen, saying:

"Now you mustn't do that, Russ! I told you that you must not!"

"What's he doing, Norah?" asked Mrs. Bunker.

"He's taking forks from the table and tying them on his shoes," answered the cook.

"You mustn't do that, Russ!" exclaimed his mother. "Why are you doing such a thing? Forks on your shoes—the idea!"

"I'm playing they're spurs, Mother, like those the cowboys at Uncle Fred's ranch wear on their boots," said Russ. "Spurs are sharp and so are forks, so I thought if I tied some forks on my shoes I'd have spurs like the cowboys."

His mother laughed, but told him that forks did not look much like spurs and, moreover, that she did not want to have her forks used for that purpose.

So Russ had to take off his fork-spurs, much to his sorrow. But he soon found something else to play with, and went about whistling merrily.

Two days before the two weeks were up Mrs. Bunker said that all the packing was done, and that she was ready to start for the West with the six little Bunkers. Meanwhile Uncle Fred and Daddy Bunker had been kept busy; the ranchman attending to his business matters, and talking with engineers about his mysterious spring, and Mr. Bunker working at his real estate affairs.

"They tell me to take some photographs of the spring and

Laura Lee Hope

send them to them," said Uncle Fred. "So I'll do that. I've bought a camera, and we'll take pictures for the engineers."

"I can do that for you," remarked Daddy Bunker. "I often take pictures of the houses I buy and sell."

The last valise and trunk had been packed. Once more the Bunker house was closed for a long vacation and the family was on the porch, waiting for the big automobile that was to take them and Uncle Fred to the station.

"Are we all here?" asked Mother Bunker, "counting noses," as she did before the start of every trip. "Oh, where's Margy?" she suddenly cried, as she did not see her little girl. "Margy isn't here! Where can she be?"

For Margy, who had been there a little while before, was missing.

## CHAPTER VI

## OFF FOR THE WEST

"Come on! Everybody hunt for Margy!" called Mr. Bunker. "She can't be very far away, as I saw her on the porch a little while ago."

"We haven't much time if we are to catch the train," said Mother Bunker. "Oh, dear! I wish she wouldn't run off that way. Did you see her go, Rose?"

"No, Mother, I didn't. But I'll go and look, and—"

"No, you stay here," said Daddy Bunker. "First we know you'll be getting lost, Rose. Uncle Fred and I will look for Margy. The rest of you stay here."

"I know where Margy goed!" suddenly exclaimed Mun Bun.

"Where?" asked Daddy and Mother Bunker and Uncle Fred. "Where did Margy go?"

"She goed to say good-bye to Carlo!"

"What! Carlo, the dog next door?" asked Mother Bunker.

"Yep!" and Mun Bun nodded his head.

"I wonder if she has," murmured Daddy Bunker. "And yet I wouldn't be surprised. The children think as much of Carlo as if he was their own dog," he said to Uncle Fred.

"Well, let's go and look," suggested the ranchman.

Back to the yard next door hurried the two men. In the rear was a nice, cosy dog-house into which Carlo went when it was cold or rainy.

"Look!" cried Uncle Fred, pointing toward the dog kennel. "There she is!"

Something pink and white was fluttering from Carlo's little house, and pink and white was the color of Margy's dress. Mr. Bunker ran down the yard.

"Margy!" he cried, as he took his little girl out from the kennel, where she was snuggled up to Carlo, her head pillowed on his shaggy coat. "Margy! what are you doing?"

"I was saying good-bye to Carlo, Daddy," the little girl answered. "I love him just bushels, and I'm going away from him, so I said good-bye!"

"Well, we might say good-bye to the train if you stayed here much longer," laughed her father, brushing the straw off the little girl's dress.

"Good-bye, Carlo! Good-bye!" called Margy, as her father carried her away.

"Bow-wow!" barked the big dog.

That was his way of saying good-bye, I suppose.

Out of the yard, into which she had gone when no one was watching her, Margy was carried by her father. Then along came the big automobile, and in that the six little Bunkers, with their daddy and mother and their Uncle Fred, rode to the station. Some of their neighbors came out on their steps to wave good-bye to the Bunkers, and Norah and Jerry Simms shook their hands and wished them the best of luck.

"Bring me back an Indian, Russ!" called Jerry.

"I'll lasso one for you," Russ answered.

"And I'll think up a lot of new riddles for you, Norah!" said Laddie.

"Sure, and I'll like that!" exclaimed the cook.

And so the six little Bunkers were off for the West.

It was a long journey from their home in Pennsylvania to Uncle Fred's ranch in Montana. It would take four days and nights of riding in railroad trains, but I am not going to tell you all that happened on the trip.

In fact nothing very much did happen. The children sat in their seats and looked out of the windows. Now and then they walked up and down the car, or asked for drinks of water. They looked at picture books, and played with games that Uncle Fred and Daddy Bunker bought for them from the train boy.

At night they all went to sleep in the car where beds were made out of what were seats in the daytime. It was not the first time the six little Bunkers had traveled in sleeping-cars, so they were not much surprised to see the colored porter make a bed out of a seat.

I will tell you about one funny thing that happened on the trip, and then I'll make the rest of the story about the things that took place on Uncle Fred's ranch, for there the children had many adventures.

"This is our last night of travel," said Mother Bunker to the children one evening, as the berths were being made up.

"Shall we be at Uncle Fred's ranch in the morning?" asked Russ, who, with Laddie, had been counting the hours when they might begin to lasso something.

"No, not exactly in the morning," said Uncle Fred himself. "But when you wake up, to-morrow morning, you can say: 'We'll be there to-night.' For by this time to-morrow night, if all goes well, we'll be at Three Star."

"Then can I see the ponies?" asked Violet.

"Yes, and have a ride on one if you want to," her uncle told her. "There are some very gentle ones that will just do for you children."

"That will be lovely!" exclaimed Rose. "I'll give my doll a ride, too."

"So will I," decided Violet.

They had taken with them their Japanese dolls, that had been found in such a funny way on the beach, as I told you in the book called "Six Little Bunkers at Cousin Tom's."

"The  berths  are ready, sir," said the colored porter to Daddy

Bunker, and soon the children were undressed and put to sleep in the queer beds for the last time on this journey.

The grown folk stayed up a bit later, talking about different things, and the queer spring on Uncle Fred's ranch.

"I hope I can find the men who have been taking my cattle," said the Westerner, as he got ready for his berth, as the beds in the sleeping-car are called.

"We'll help you find the bad chaps," said Daddy Bunker.

"And the children will want to help, too," added Mrs. Bunker. "Especially Russ and Laddie. They think they are getting to be quite big boys now. They may find out what is the matter with your spring, Fred."

"I hope they do, but I don't see how they can," answered the ranchman. "I've tried every way I know, and so have my cowboys. Well, we'll wait until we get out to the ranch, and then see what happens."

Pretty soon every one in the big sleeping-car was in bed. The Bunkers, two by two, were sleeping in the berths. Russ and Laddie were together in one, and Rose and Violet were in another. Mun Bun slept with his father, and Margy with her mother.

On and on rushed the train through the night, carrying the people farther West. The weather was fine now, and spring would soon give place to summer. Uncle Fred had said this was the nicest time of the year out on his ranch.

It must have been about the middle of the night that Mr. Bunker awakened suddenly. Just what caused him to do so he did not know, but he found himself wide awake in a moment. He reached over to see if Mun Bun was all right, and, to his surprise, he could not find his little son.

"That's queer!" exclaimed Mr. Bunker to himself. "Where can Mun Bun be? I wonder if he got up in the night to get himself a drink?"

The little fellow had never done this, but that is not saying he might not try it for the first time.

"Or perhaps he didn't like it in bed with me, and went in with his mother and Margy," thought Mr. Bunker.

Mrs. Bunker's berth was right across the aisle from the one in which Mr. Bunker had been sleeping with Mun Bun, and, putting on a bath robe, Mr. Bunker pushed back the curtains in front of his berth, and opened those of the one where his wife was sleeping.

"Amy! Amy!" he whispered, his lips close to her ear so as not to awaken the other passengers on either side. "Amy! is Mun Bun here with you?"

"What's the matter?" asked Mrs. Bunker, waking up suddenly.

"I woke up just now and I can't find Mun Bun. Is he in here?"

# CHAPTER VII

## AT THREE STAR RANCH

But as Mr. Bunker parted the curtains over his wife's berth, and looked inside, he saw, by the dim light that streamed in, that Mun Bun was not with her. There was Margy, quietly sleeping with her mother, but no Mun Bun.

"What could have happened to him?" asked Mrs. Bunker, sitting up in bed. She looked at her husband. "Where is Mun Bun?" she asked.

"I don't know," he answered. "He was sleeping with me, but, all of a sudden, I woke up and Mun Bun was not with me."

"He must have awakened and got up to get a drink, or something," said Mrs. Bunker. "Then when he went to go back again, he couldn't find the place where you were, and he's either crawled in with Russ and Laddie, or with Rose and Violet. We must look for him."

"I'll look," said Mr. Bunker. "You stay with Margy. If she wakes up and finds you gone, she'll cry and disturb the whole car. You stay here, and I'll go and look in the two other berths."

Going along the aisle of the car, which was swaying to and fro from the speed of the train, Mr. Bunker softly opened the curtains of the berth next to that in which his wife and Margy were. In this second compartment were Violet and Rose.

It needed only a glance to show that Mun Bun was not with his sisters, though often, at home, when he had been disturbed in the night, he had been found in their bed.

"Well, I'll try where Laddie and Russ are sleeping," said Mr. Bunker. "He surely will be there."

But Mun Bun was not in the berth with Russ and Laddie.

Rather puzzled, and not knowing exactly what to do next, Mr. Bunker went back to his wife's berth. She was sitting up waiting for him, and Margy was still asleep.

"Did you find him?" whispered Mrs. Bunker.

"No, he wasn't with Russ or Rose. What shall I do?"

Just then the colored porter came along. He had seen Mr. Bunker roving around the car, and wanted to know if there was any trouble. The porter was supposed to stay awake all night, but he often went to sleep, though he did not undress.

"Is there anything the matter, sir?" he asked Mr. Bunker.

"Well, it's a queer thing, but my little boy, who was sleeping with me, is missing," said Mr. Bunker. "I woke up to find him gone."

"Is he in the berths where any of the rest of your family are sleeping?" asked the porter, for, having traveled with the Bunkers for some time, he knew them all, at least by sight.

"No, he isn't in with his sisters or brothers," answered Mr. Bunker.

"Oh, you didn't look in Fred's berth!" exclaimed Mrs. Bunker. "That's where he is, Charles. I'm sure."

"Very likely," said Mr. Bunker, a sound of relief in his voice. "I didn't think of looking there!"

It was only a few steps to the berth where Uncle Fred was sleeping by himself, and when Daddy Bunker pulled open the curtains there, he at once awakened his wife's brother.

"What is it? What's the matter? Has there been an accident—a smash-up?" asked the Westerner quickly.

"No, nothing has happened except that Mun Bun is lost and we can't find him," answered Mr. Bunker in a low voice, so as not to disturb the other passengers. "I thought maybe he had crawled in with you, as he isn't with Amy, nor with Russ nor Rose."

"He isn't here," said Uncle Fred. "I'd have felt him if he had come into my berth. I'll get up and help you look."

Uncle Fred quickly slipped on a bath robe and stepped out into the aisle of the car. Then he and Daddy Bunker and the porter stood there in the dim light.

"Did you find him, Charles?" asked Mrs. Bunker in a low voice from her berth.

"No, he wasn't with Fred."

"Oh, dear! What shall we do? You must find him!" she exclaimed, as she poked her head out between the curtains.

"Well, ma'am, he couldn't fall off the train," said the porter, "'cause we hasn't stopped for a long while, and the doors are tight closed at each end of the car. He's here somewhere."

"He's in some other berth," put in Uncle Fred. "He must have walked in his sleep, or something like that, and he's in with some one else he has mistaken for his father or his mother, or one of his sisters or brothers. We'll find him."

"But we can't wake up everybody in the car, to ask them if Mun Bun is sleeping with them," said Mr. Bunker.

"We've just got to!" exclaimed his wife. "We must find Mun Bun!"

The porter looked disturbed. He did not very much like to awaken all the sleeping passengers in the train, for some of them were sure to be cross. They might blame him for their loss of sleep, and then he would not get the usual tips of quarters or half dollars or dollars at the end of the ride.

"I'll tell you what we can do," said Uncle Fred.

"What?" asked Daddy Bunker.

"Since we know Mun Bun is safe in this car, as the porter says he couldn't get off, we can wait until morning. He surely is in some berth, and is, very likely, sleeping soundly. Why not let him alone until morning?" answered Uncle Fred.

"Oh, no! Never!" cried Mrs. Bunker. "I must have him found, even if we have to wake up everybody in the train. I must find Mun Bun!"

Once more the porter hesitated.

"Well, if it has to be done, it has to be," he said. "I'll start at one end, an' you two gen'mens can start at the other end of the car, and maybe we won't have to wake up quite everybody."

Just as they were going to start to make this search a voice from behind the colored porter called.

"Are you looking for a lost boy?" inquired a man who wore an old-fashioned night-cap on his head, which he stuck out from between the green curtains of his berth.

"Yes!" eagerly exclaimed Mr. Bunker.

"Have you one there?" asked Uncle Fred, turning to look at the man.

"Well, I have some sort of a youngster in my berth with me," was the low, laughing answer. "I had a dream that my pet dog had climbed in bed with me, as he sometimes does when I'm at home. In my sleep I put out my hand and I felt some soft, curly head. Then I happened to think, in my dream, that my dog is an Airedale, and they don't exactly have soft, silky hair.

"Then I woke up, reached under my pillow for my flash-light, and pressed the switch. There I saw a small boy asleep with me. Maybe he's the one you want."

"Oh, it must be Mun Bun!" exclaimed Mrs. Bunker. "Look quick, Charles!"

Mr. Bunker went down to the berth whence the man with the night-cap had spoken. There, surely enough, peacefully sleeping in the strange bed, was Mun Bun.

"Yes, that's my boy," said Daddy Bunker. "Sorry he bothered you."

"Shucks, he didn't bother me a mite!" said the good-natured man. "I used to have a little tot like him myself, but he's grown up now, and gone to war. I'm old and bald-headed— that's why I wear this night-cap, on account of my bald head," he went on. "But I'm not too old to like children. You can let him stay here until morning if you wish. He won't bother me."

"No, thank you," said Mr. Bunker. "He might wake up and be frightened if he found himself in a strange bed. I'll carry him back with me. Thank you just the same."

Daddy Bunker picked up Mun Bun, still sleeping, and the little fellow never awakened. His father took him back to his own berth. Uncle Fred got into his and Mrs. Bunker went back to sleep beside Margy.

Mun Bun never awakened as his father carried him back, but slept on. Only he murmured something in his dreams about "pony rides."

"You shall have some when you get to Uncle Fred's ranch," whispered Daddy Bunker, as he softly kissed the little sleeping fellow. And Mun Bun was once more tucked in the bed where he belonged.

In the morning the other little Bunkers were told of the funny thing that had happened to Mun Bun in the night. The little fellow himself knew nothing about it.

"He must have walked in his sleep," said his mother, "though I never knew him to do that before."

And that is probably what happened.

Mun Bun, not used to sleeping in moving trains, had probably twisted and turned in the night, and, being restless, he had gotten out of the bed where he was with his father. If he was awake he did not remember it. He must have toddled down the aisle of the car, all by himself, and then have crawled into the berth with the strange man. The latter was not awakened until he had his queer dream about his pet dog, and then he found Mun Bun.

"And just in time, too," said Uncle Fred, as they were all laughing about it at breakfast the next morning. "I wouldn't have liked to get all the passengers awake to find a lost boy. After this, Mun Bun, we'll have to put a hobble on you."

"What's a hobble?" asked Russ.

"Is it an Indian?" Violet wanted to know. She was not going to let Russ get ahead of her with questions.

"No, a hobble is something we put on horses to keep them from straying away," said the ranchman. "It's a rope with which we tie them."

"Do horses walk in their sleep?" Violet, in wonder, asked.

"I don't believe so," answered Uncle Fred. "I never saw any, and we have a lot out at Three Star."

"Why don't they?" asked Violet, after a pause.

"Why don't they what?" her uncle queried, for he had turned aside and was talking to Daddy Bunker.

"Why don't horses walk in their sleep?" asked Violet. "Mun

Bun walked in his sleep, so why don't horses?"

"Oh, I guess they do enough walking and running in the day time," said Mrs. Bunker. "They're glad enough to rest at night."

"I guess I'll make up a riddle about Mun Bun walking in his sleep, if I can think of a good answer," announced Laddie.

"Do!" exclaimed Uncle Fred. "And save it for the cowboys out at my ranch. They like riddles."

"Do they?" cried Laddie. "Then I'll ask them that one about what do the tickets do when the conductor punches them. Nobody can tell me an answer to that."

"Yes, that would be a good one for the cowboys," laughed Uncle Fred. "Well, it won't be very long before we'll be there now."

The train sped on, and late that afternoon Moon City was reached. It was a small town, but it had the name of being a city. The children did not have much time to look about, as Uncle Fred was anxious to get them out to the ranch.

So, with bags and trunks, the Bunkers were piled into a big four-seated wagon, or buckboard, and the horses started off. Through the town they went, and then out on the broad plains. In the distance were great mountains and forests.

It was a drive of about ten miles to Three Star Ranch, and it was just getting dusk when the place was reached.

"Welcome home, six little Bunkers!" cried Uncle Fred, as he jumped from the wagon and began helping down his sister and the children. "Here we are, at my ranch at last."

"Where are the Indians?" asked Russ eagerly.

And just then came wild yells and whoops, and the air resounded with the firing of what the children thought must be giant fire-crackers, bigger than any they had ever heard.

"Whoop-ee! Whoop! Bang! Bang!" sounded on all sides.

# CHAPTER VIII

## RUSS MAKES A LASSO

There was so much noise that, at first, no one could make his or her voice heard. Then, as the sound of the shooting died away a little, and the whoops and shouts were not so loud, Laddie cried:

"Is that the Indians, Uncle Fred? Are they trying to get us?"

"Where's my lasso?" demanded Russ. "I had one on the train! Where is it, Mother? I want to lasso an Indian for Jerry Simms."

"Can't the cowboys help fight the Indians?" demanded Laddie, capering about in his excitement.

"Oh, look!" suddenly exclaimed Rose, and she pointed to a lot of men on horses coming around the corner of the big ranch house.

And as the children looked, these men again fired their big revolvers in the air, making such a racket that Mother Bunker covered her ears with her hands.

"Oh, here come the cowboys!" yelled Russ. "Now the

Indians will run!"

"Let me see the cowboys! Let me see the cowboys!" cried Mun Bun. "Has they got any cows?"

Right up to where the six little Bunkers stood rode the cowboys on their horses, or "ponies," as they are more often called. Then the men suddenly pulled back on the reins, and up in the air on their hind legs stood the horses, the men clinging to their backs, swinging their big hats and yelling as loudly as they could.

"Oh, it's just like a circus!" cried Rose.

"Indeed it is," said her father. "More like a Wild West circus, I suppose."

"Did you get this show up for us, Fred?" asked Mother Bunker, when the cowboys had quieted down, and had ridden off to the corral, or place where they kept their horses.

"No, I didn't know anything about it," answered Uncle Fred. "But the cowboys often ride wild like that when they come in from their work and find visitors. They shoot off their revolvers, 'guns,' as they call them, and make as much noise as they can."

"What for?" asked Violet.

"Oh, just because they feel good, and they want to make everybody else feel good, too, I suppose."

"Will the Indians come?" asked Laddie hopefully.

"No, there aren't any Indians," his uncle told him. "At least not any around here now. Sometimes a few come from the reservation, but there's none here now."

The six little Bunkers watched the cowboys ride away to put their horses out to grass and wash themselves for supper, or "grub," or "chuck," or "chow," as they called it, giving the meals different names used according to the place where they had worked before.

"I'm glad they weren't Indians," said Laddie to Russ, as they went in the ranch house where Uncle Fred lived.

"Pooh! I wasn't afraid!" said Russ.

"No, I wasn't either," went on Laddie. "But I don't like Indians to come at you the first thing. I was glad they were cowboys."

"If they'd've been Indians I'd've lassoed 'em!" declared Russ.

"How could you, when you didn't have a lasso?"

"I'm going to make one," declared Russ.

"I'll help you lasso," offered Laddie.

"Pooh! you don't know how," said Russ. "But I'll teach you," he added.

"Come in and wash yourselves for supper," called Mother Bunker to the two boys, who had stayed out on the porch to see if the cowboys would again ride their horses around so wildly and shoot off the guns which made so much noise. "You must be hungry, Russ and Laddie."

"I am," Laddie admitted.

"So'm I," agreed Russ.

Into Uncle Fred's ranch house went all six little Bunkers. They liked the place from the very first. It was different from their house at home.

The room they went into first extended the width of the house. It was "big enough for the whole Bunker family and part of another one to sit in, and not rock on one anothers' toes," Mother Bunker said. Back of this big apartment, called the living-room, was the dining-room. Then came the kitchen, and, off in another part of the house, were the sleeping-rooms. The ranch house was only one story high, and it was, in fact, a sort of bungalow. It was very nice.

Even though it was away out on the plains Uncle Fred's house had some of the same things in it that the Bunkers had at home. There was running water, and a bathroom, and a sink in the kitchen.

"The water comes from the mysterious spring I told you about," said Uncle Fred when Mrs. Bunker asked him about it. "We pump it up into a tank with a gasolene engine pump, and then it runs into the bathroom or wherever else we want it. Oh, we'll treat you all right out here, you'll see!"

"I'm sure you will," said Mother Bunker.

The children were washed and combed after their long journey, and then Uncle Fred led them out to the dining-room.

"Who does your cooking?" asked Mrs. Bunker.

"Bill Johnson," was the answer. "He's a fine cook, too."

"Is he a *man*?" asked Rose, in some surprise.

"When you see him you'll say so!" exclaimed her uncle. "Bill is about six feet tall, and as thin as a rail. But he certainly can cook."

"I didn't think a *man* could cook," went on Rose.

"Of course they can!" laughed her father. "You ought to see me cook when I go camping and fishing. And the cook we had in the train coming here was a man."

"Was he?" asked Rose. "How funny!"

"Here he comes now," said Uncle Fred, as a tall, thin man, wearing a white apron and a cap came into the room with a big tray balanced on his hands. "Bill, this little girl thinks you can't cook because you're a man!"

"Oh, I only said—I only said—" and Rose blushed and hung her head.

"That's all right!" laughed Bill Johnson. "If she doesn't like my cooking I'll have her come out and show me how to make a pie or a cake!" and he laughed at Rose.

But the six little Bunkers all agreed that they never had a better meal than that first one at Uncle Fred's, even if it was cooked by a man who used to be a cowboy, as he told them later.

"It was as good as Grandma Bell's," said Russ.

"And as good as Aunt Jo's," added Rose.

"I'm glad we came!" declared Laddie, as he pulled a cookie

out of his pocket. He had taken it away with him from the table.

After supper the children and grown folk walked around the ranch near the house. They saw where the cowboys slept in the "bunk house," and looked in the corral where the ponies were kept when they were not being ridden.

"Where are the little ponies we are to ride?" asked Rose of her uncle.

"I'll show them to you to-morrow," he promised. "It's too far to go over to their corral to-night."

"Will the cowboys shoot any more?" Laddie wanted to know.

"No, not to-night," said his father. "I guess they want a rest as much as you children do."

Indeed the six little Bunkers were very willing to go to bed that night. They were tired with their long journey, and sleeping in a regular bed was different from curling up in a berth made from seats in a car. Even Mun Bun slept soundly, and did not walk in his sleep and get in bed with any one else.

Early in the morning the children were down to breakfast. They found that Bill Johnson could get that sort of meal just as well as he could cook a supper, and after taking plenty of milk and oatmeal, with some bread and jam, the six little Bunkers were ready to have some fun.

They had on their play clothes, for the trunks and valises had been unpacked, and as the weather was mild, though it was not quite summer yet, they could play out of doors as much as they liked.

"I'm going to look at the cowboys," announced Russ, as he got up from the table. "I want to see how they lasso."

"So do I," said Laddie.

"Then you'll have to wait a bit, boys," Uncle Fred told them. "The cowboys have ridden over to the far end of the ranch to see about some cattle. They won't be back until evening."

"Could we walk over and see 'em?" asked Russ. "I want to see how they lasso."

"Well, it's several miles to where they have gone," said Uncle Fred. "I'm afraid you couldn't walk it. But you can go almost anywhere else you like, as there's no danger around here."

"Are there any wild bulls or steers or cows that might chase them?" asked Mother Bunker.

"No," answered her brother. "There are a few little calves in a pen out near the barn, but that's all. The cattle and horses are far away."

"Let's go out and see this mysterious spring of yours," said Daddy Bunker. "I'm eager to have a look at it. I'll take the camera along and get some pictures. Come, children!"

Rose and Violet, with Margy and Mun Bun, followed their father and mother and Uncle Fred. Laddie and Russ lagged behind.

"Aren't you coming?" asked their mother.

"I'm going to make a lasso," said Russ.

"So'm I," added Laddie.

"Oh, let them play by themselves," said Uncle Fred. "They can't do any damage nor come to any harm. They can see the spring later."

So Russ and Laddie went off by themselves to make a lasso. Russ found a piece of clothesline, which Bill Johnson, the cook, said he might take, and soon Russ and his brother were tying knots and loops in the strong cord.

If you don't know what a lasso or lariat is I'll tell you. It is just a long rope with what is known as a slip-knot in one end. That end is thrown over a horse, a cow, or anything else you want to catch. The loop, or noose, slips along the long part of the string, and is pulled tight. Then the horse or cow can be held and kept from getting away.

Mother and Daddy Bunker, with the four little Bunkers and Uncle Fred, were looking at the queer spring, which I'll tell you about a little later, when Laddie came running up to them.

"What's the matter?" asked Uncle Fred, seeing that the small boy seemed excited.

"Russ made—made a lasso," panted Laddie, for he had been running, and was out of breath.

"Yes, I know he said he was going to," said Uncle Fred. "That's all right. Have a good time with it."

"Russ made—made a lasso, and he—he lassoed one of the little cows with it!" went on Laddie.

"Oh, did he!" exclaimed Mr. Bell with a laugh. "Well, I guess what little lassoing Russ can do won't hurt the calf. They are all pretty well grown."

"But Russ can't—can't get loose!" went on Laddie. "He's yelling like anything and he says I'd better come and tell you! He lassoed the calf but he can't get loose—I mean Russ can't get loose!"

"Oh, my goodness!" exclaimed Mrs. Bunker. "I might have known something would happen!"

# CHAPTER IX

## THE QUEER SPRING

"What's all this? What's the matter?" asked Daddy Bunker, who had been looking at the mysterious spring and had not heard all the talk that went on. "What happened?"

"Russ made a lasso," stated Laddie, while Mrs. Bunker and Uncle Fred started for the corral where the little calves were kept until they were strong enough to run with the other cattle.

"Oh, Russ made a lasso, did he?" asked his father. "Well, that boy is always making something. He'll be an inventor yet, I'm sure."

"Russ lassoed a calf," explained Mrs. Bunker, for Mr. Bunker had caught up Laddie, and they had now overtaken the others, who had started on ahead.

"Well, he had to lasso something," said Mr. Bunker with a laugh. "Any boy wants to lasso something when he makes a lariat. I did when I was a boy. I lassoed our old rooster."

"But the trouble seems to be," said Uncle Fred, "that Russ lassoed a calf, and now the calf is running away with Russ."

"Oh, that's different!" said Mr. Bunker. "We'll have to see about this!"

Then he hurried along with his wife and Uncle Fred toward the calf corral. The five little Bunkers stayed behind at the spring for Mrs. Bunker called back to them to do this, sending Laddie back, too.

"We don't want any of them to get into trouble," she said to her brother.

"Yes, I think, too, that one at a time is enough," replied Mr. Bell.

Even before they reached the corral they heard the voice of Russ yelling. They heard him calling:

"Whoa now! Stop! Stop, bossy cow! Let me get up! Stop!"

"Maybe the calf will hook him!" cried Mrs. Bunker.

"Oh, no!" answered Uncle Fred. "The calves don't have horns. Russ will be all right, though he may be mussed up a bit."

"It will teach him not to lasso calves after this," said Mr. Bunker.

"I'm not so sure of that," murmured Mrs. Bunker. "It is more apt to make the others want to try the same thing."

A moment later they turned around the corner of one of the ranch buildings and came in sight of the corral. In one end they could see some frightened calves standing huddled together. In the middle of the corral was a cloud of dust.

"That must be Russ and the calf," said Uncle Fred.

He and Daddy Bunker ran faster toward the fence, within which the calves were kept, but, before they could reach it, they saw a man run out from one of the buildings, jump over the fence without touching it and land inside the corral. Then he disappeared in the cloud of dust.

A moment later he came out, carrying Russ in his arms, and from the little boy's leg there dangled a piece of clothesline. Then, also out of the dust cloud, came a very much frightened spotted calf, and around its neck was another piece of line.

"Oh, is he—is he hurt?" gasped Mrs. Bunker, for Russ was limp.

"Not a bit, I'm glad to say!" answered the man who had Russ in his arms. "He's pretty dusty, and scratched up a bit, and his clothes are mussed, and he's frightened, but he's not hurt; are you?" and he laughed as he set Russ down on his own feet.

"I—I guess I'm all right," Russ answered, a bit slowly. "I—I had a dandy time!"

"Well, I should say you did!" exclaimed his father. "What did you do?"

"Well, I was playing I was a cowboy in the Wild West and I lassoed a buffalo. I made believe the calf was a buffalo."

"And then I guess the calf made believe you were a football, by the way it pulled you about the corral," said the man who had rescued Russ.

"Yes, sir, I guess so," answered Russ.

"I'm glad you rescued him," said Mrs. Bunker to the stranger. "I can't thank you enough."

"Oh, I didn't do anything," was the answer. "I heard the little fellow yelling shortly after I had seen him in the corral with the piece of clothesline. I guessed what had happened, and I jumped in. I found the calf pulling him around, for the lasso the little boy made had gotten tangled around his legs. The other end was on the calf.

"So I just cut the rope and picked up the youngster. Here he is, not much worse for wear. But you won't do it again, will you?"

"No—no—I don't guess I will," answered Russ.

"Captain Roy, this is my sister, Mrs. Bunker, and this is Mr. Bunker," said Uncle Fred, introducing them. "This is Captain Robert Roy, my ranch partner about whom I spoke to you," he went on to Mr. and Mrs. Bunker. "He has been away, or you would have met him last night."

"I'm glad you are here to-day, to get my boy out of the trouble he got himself into," said Mr. Bunker, as he shook hands with the former soldier.

"I am glad, too!" exclaimed the captain. "I like children, and I don't want to see them hurt. But, as it happened, Russ wasn't."

"He might have been, only for you," said Mrs. Bunker. "We can't thank you enough. Russ, don't lasso anything more."

"Can't I lasso a fence post, Mother?" Russ asked.

"Well, maybe that, or something that isn't alive. But no more calves."

"All right," said Russ.

His clothes were brushed off, Captain Roy talked a little while with Mr. and Mrs. Bunker, and then went back to his work, and Uncle Fred remarked:

"Well, now the excitement is over, we can go back to the spring. I presume the other children will be wondering what has happened."

So back they went to where Laddie, Rose and the others were waiting.

"Did you get him?" asked Laddie eagerly, when he saw Russ.

"No, he got me," was the answer. "I guess we won't play Wild West any more. We'll be Indians and not cowboys. Indians don't have to lasso buffaloes, do they, Uncle Fred."

"No, Indians have it sort of easy out here on their reservation," said Mr. Bell with a laugh. "I guess it will be safer for you boys to be Indians."

"That'll be fun too," agreed Russ.

"But we must have some feathers for our heads," said Laddie.

"We can get them in the chicken yard," returned Russ.

"Did the calf bite you?" asked Violet, and she looked at Russ as if to make sure he was all there.

"No, he didn't bite, but he almost stepped on me. You ought to have seen me flying around the field on the end of the rope. I couldn't get it loose," and Russ explained how it had happened.

However he was well out of it, and promised never again to try such a trick.

"I could make a riddle up about it, but I'm not going to," said Laddie. "Anyhow it's hard to guess the answer, so I'll think up one that's easier."

"Now this," said Uncle Fred, as they stood about the big spring, "is what I was telling you about. You all see what a nice lot of water there is here. Sometimes it overflows, there's so much. Then, within a few hours, it will go dry."

"And where does the water go?" asked Daddy Bunker.

"That's what none of us has been able to find out. The water just seems to sink down into the ground, as if the bottom had dropped out and let it all through. Then again, in a day or so, the water comes back again."

"It is queer," said Mrs. Bunker.

"And the worst of it is," said Uncle Fred, "that I may lose most of what I put into this ranch on account of this spring."

"How?" asked Daddy Bunker.

"Well, I bought this ranch partly because it had such a fine spring of water on it. There is none better for miles around. But if I wanted to sell the ranch again, and people heard that the spring went dry every now and then, they wouldn't pay me as much as I paid. So I would lose. That's one reason why

I'm so anxious to get to the bottom of the puzzle. As I said, it's like one of Laddie's riddles—I don't know the answer."

"It looks like a regular spring," said Mother Bunker.

"And yet it isn't," went on Uncle Fred. "It's all right now, but an hour later we may find the water sinking away."

"I'll take some pictures," said Daddy Bunker, who had a camera with him, "and then maybe we can dig up the ground and find hidden pipes, or something like that."

"We'll do the digging to-morrow," said Uncle Fred. "Now I want to show you about the ranch."

So he led them about, showing the six little Bunkers and their father and mother the different buildings, telling them how he raised his cattle and sent them to market, and how he sent out his cowboys to hunt for lost calves.

"There's always something to do on a ranch like this," said Uncle Fred. "You can keep busy all the while. If one thing doesn't happen another will. What with the mysterious spring, the bad men taking my cattle now and then, the Indians running off the reservation and making trouble—well, you can keep busy."

"Could we see the little ponies?" asked Rose. "I'd like to have a ride on one."

"So would I!" exclaimed Russ. "I'd like a pony better than a calf."

"The ponies are over this way. I'll show them to you," said Uncle Fred. "We'll go back by way of the spring. I have some Shetland ponies," he went on to Daddy Bunker. "I raised a few and may raise more. The larger children can ride on them while they're at the ranch."

"That will be fine!" exclaimed Mrs. Bunker. "Oh, I'm sure the children will love it here."

They turned back toward the spring to go to the pony corral.

"I'm thirsty!" exclaimed Russ, as they reached the water hole. "I'm going to run on ahead and get a drink."

On he ran, and the others saw him stop suddenly when he reached the spring. Then Russ shouted:

"Oh, come here! Come here quick! Look! Hurry!"

# CHAPTER X

## SOME BAD NEWS

"I wonder what the matter is," said Mrs. Bunker, when she heard Russ shout.

She did not have to wonder long. As the others drew nearer, Russ shouted again, and this time he said:

"The water's all running out of the spring! It's going dry, just like Uncle Fred said it would!"

"More mystery!" exclaimed the ranchman as he hurried on.

The five little Bunkers and the grown folk reached the edge of the big spring where Russ stood. He was looking down into the clear water, and the others did the same.

"Surely enough, it is getting lower!" exclaimed Mother Bunker.

"There isn't half as much in as there was at first," added her husband. "Is this the way it always does, Fred?"

"I never saw it run out before," answered the owner of Three Star Ranch. "Every time before, it has happened in the night when no one was near it. We'd visit the spring in the evening, and it would be all right. In the morning it would be nearly dry, and it might stay that way a day or two before the water came back into it. Very queer, I call it."

"So do I!" exclaimed Daddy Bunker. "I'll take another picture of it now. Maybe that will help us solve the mystery."

While he was getting the camera ready Mrs. Bunker said:

"The water is going out fast. You'd better get a drink now, Russ dear, if you want it, for there may not be any more for a long time."

"I will!" exclaimed Russ.

Uncle Fred kept half a cocoanut shell tied by a string near the spring to use as a cup. This Russ dipped in the fast lowering water, and got a drink for the other little Bunkers and for himself, as they all seemed to be thirsty at once.

"What will you do for water when the spring runs dry?" asked Mrs. Bunker of her brother.

"We'll have to draw some from the creek, but I have a lot of this water stored in the tank. I always keep that full lately, since I can't tell when my spring is going dry."

They stood and watched the water going out of the spring. It was just like it is when you pull the stopper out of the bathtub. The water gets lower and lower, running down the pipe. Only, of course, there was no pipe in the spring—that is, as far as Uncle Fred knew.

"The water seems just to stop running in," said Daddy Bunker, as he knelt down and looked more closely at the little hill of rocks back of the water hole. It was from cracks in these rocks that the water bubbled out and filled a hollow, rock basin before flowing on. Now less and less was coming and, of course, as the spring water always kept running away, or it would have overflowed, the basin was slowly but surely getting dry.

"I think what is happening," said Daddy Bunker, "is that, somewhere back in the mountains or hills, where the stream comes from that feeds this spring, the water is being shut off, just as we shut off the water at the kitchen sink faucet. Where does the water come from, Fred?"

"I don't know," was the answer. "It must come from some place underground, as we've never been able to find it on top. Well, we won't go thirsty, for there is plenty of water in the tank. But I hope the spring soon fills up again."

Even as they watched the water got lower and lower, until there was hardly a pailful left in the rock basin. No more clear, sparkling water bubbled up out of the cracks in the rocks. The strange thing that Uncle Fred had told about was happening at the spring.

"Is the cows drinking up all the water?" asked Mun Bun, as he looked into the now almost emptied basin.

"No, I don't believe they are," answered his uncle.

"Maybe the Indians took it to wash in," said Margy. "The Indians wash, doesn't they, Uncle Fred?"

"Well, maybe some of 'em do, but not very often," was the answer. "They're not very fond of water, I'm sorry to say. But there! we won't worry about this any more. You six little Bunkers came here to have fun, and not bother about my spring. Daddy and I will try to find out why the water runs away, and stop the leak. Did you all get drinks? If you did we'll go back to the house. It must be almost dinner time."

They all had had enough to drink for the time being, and, leaving the spring, which was now only a damp hole in the ground, the party went back to the ranch house. Captain Roy met them.

"Spring's gone dry again," said Uncle Fred.

"Again! That's too bad! I was hoping we'd seen the last of that. Well, now, we may expect some more bad news."

"What kind?" asked Mrs. Bunker.

"Oh, the captain means about losing more cattle," answered Uncle Fred. "Almost always, when the spring goes dry, it isn't long before some of the cowboys come in to tell about our cattle being taken away. But maybe that won't happen this time."

After dinner the six little Bunkers started to have some fun. Mun Bun and Margy went to have their afternoon naps, but Rose and Violet took their Japanese dolls, which had been unpacked, and found a shady place on the porch where they could play.

"What are you going to do, Russ?" asked Laddie, as he saw his brother with some sticks.

"I'm going to make a tent," was the answer. "We can make a tent and live in it same as the Indians do. It's more fun to live in a tent than in a house when you're out West."

"Oh, yes!" cried Laddie. "I'll help you. But where can we get the cloth part?"

"Well, I got the sticks," Russ went on. "I guess Uncle Fred will let us take a sheet off the bed for the cloth part."

But the boys did not make the tent that day. Just as they were thinking about going to ask for the cloth Uncle Fred called:

"Come on, Russ and Laddie, and you, too, Rose and Vi. We're going to look at the ponies. I started to take you to them when we found the spring was going dry, and that made me forget. Now we'll go."

"Oh, what fun!" cried Russ.

"Dandy!" exclaimed Laddie.

"I love to ride a pony!" added Rose.

"So do I!" ejaculated Violet.

Uncle Fred led the children to a small corral, which they had not seen before. In it were a number of Shetland ponies, some no larger than big Newfoundland dogs. And some of the ponies came to the fence to be petted as soon as they saw Uncle Fred.

"Oh, aren't they cute!" exclaimed Rose.

"I'd like to ride that black one!" shouted Laddie.

"He's a little too wild," said Uncle Fred. "Better try one of the more gentle ones first. I'll get the men to saddle 'em for you."

In a little while the four little Bunkers were riding about on

Laura Lee Hope

the backs of four gentle ponies. The little animals seemed to know children were on their backs, and they did not run fast, nor kick up their heels.

Rose and Russ could soon manage their ponies by themselves, but as Vi and Laddie were younger Uncle Fred and one of his cowboys led their ponies about by the bridle. The children rode in a big field, with a fence all around it.

"Now I'm going to ride fast!" cried Russ as he took a tighter hold of the reins and shook his feet in the stirrups. "Giddap!" he called to his pony. "Go fast!"

Maybe the pony was surprised at this. Anyhow, he started to gallop. Now Russ was not as good a horseman as he supposed, and the first he knew he had slipped from the saddle and fallen off.

"There you go!" cried Uncle Fred, as he left the pony on which Vi was riding and ran to help Russ.

Russ had fallen in a bunch of soft grass, so he was not hurt; and the pony, after trotting around in a circle, stood still and began to eat grass.

"I wouldn't try to ride fast yet a while," said Uncle Fred. "Better learn more about the ponies first. You can have just as much fun riding slowly, and then you won't tumble off."

"I won't go fast any more," said Russ, as his uncle helped him back into the saddle. The other children did not have any accidents, and rode around on the ponies for some time. Then Mun Bun and Margy awakened from their naps, and they, too, wanted rides. Their father and mother held them on the backs of two small ponies, and walked with them about the grassy field, so that all six little Bunkers had pony rides that day.

"And may we ride to-morrow?" asked Laddie when it was time to go back to the house.

"Yes," promised his uncle, "to-morrow we may all take a ride over the plain."

"Goody!" exclaimed Violet.

"Will mother come, too?" asked Rose.

"No, indeed!" laughed Mrs. Bunker. "I don't know how to ride pony-back, and I'm not going to learn now. You children can go."

"That's what we'll do then," said Uncle Fred. "Daddy and I will take Rose and Vi and Laddie and Russ for a ride over the plain. We'll go and see if we can find where our spring water comes from, and why it shuts itself off in that queer way."

The children waved good-bye to the ponies, and went back to the house. On the broad, shady porch stood Captain Roy. He was waiting for Uncle Fred, and there was a worried look on the old soldier's face.

"What's the matter?" asked the ranchman of his partner.

"More bad news," was the answer. "One of the cowboys just rode in to tell me that some more of the cattle have been taken."

"I might have known it!" cried Uncle Fred. "When the spring goes dry other bad news is sure to come in!"

# CHAPTER XI

## VIOLET TAKES A WALK

Uncle Fred seemed tired as he sat down in a chair on the porch. He looked up at Captain Roy and asked:

"How many cattle gone this time?"

"About twenty-five. One of the cowboys, who was watching them, rode over to the far end of the field to see about a steer that had fallen into a big hole and couldn't get out, and when he got back the twenty-five steers were gone."

"Hum! More work of those bad men!" exclaimed Uncle Fred. "Well, we'll see if we can catch them. Want to come along?" he asked Daddy Bunker.

"Where are you going?"

"To see if we can find the lost cattle. Maybe we can catch the men who drove them away."

"Oh, let me come!" begged Russ. "Maybe I can lasso 'em!"

"They might lasso you!" laughed his father. "No, you had better stay here. We'll soon be back."

"Oh, Daddy, please?"

"Not this time, Sonny," answered his father.

So Uncle Fred and Daddy Bunker, with some of the cow-boys, saddled their horses and started off to look for the lost cattle.

"I wish I could go!" sighed Russ, as he watched the horse-men riding off.

"So do I," echoed Laddie. "We could maybe help catch 'em. Mother, couldn't we go?"

"They'd be more likely to catch you, just as the calf did," said Mother Bunker. "Wouldn't they, Captain Roy?"

"Yes, indeed," answered the old soldier, smiling at the children. "Men who take cattle that do not belong to them are very likely to be bad men, and they would not be nice to the six little Bunkers. You stay with me, and you may come out and see the ponies again, though I won't promise you can ride on them."

"Are you going to feed them?" asked Mun Bun.

"No, they feed themselves on the grass in their field," said the captain.

"I don't like to eat grass," said Mun Bun, shaking his head.

"Neither do I," added Margy.

"Why, I do declare! I believe you're hungry," laughed Captain Roy. "And it's two hours until supper. Come on, we'll go see what Bill Johnson has in his cupboard."

"Could I come, too?" asked Russ. "I—I guess I'm hungry."

"So'm I," put in Laddie.

"Me, too!" added Violet.

"Come on, all of you!" laughed Captain Roy. "It's almost as easy to feed six as it is two," he added to Mother Bunker.

"Oh, it's too bad to bother you," she said quickly.

"No bother at all!" exclaimed the old soldier. "I know I used to want my rations when I was in the army, and I guess there isn't much difference nowadays. Come along, little Bunkers!"

Soon the children were having bread and milk, with a dish of canned peaches in addition. There were big cases of canned peaches in Bill Johnson's kitchen, and when Russ asked him why he had so many the cook said:

"Well, the boys seem to like 'em more than anything else. It's hard to get fresh fruit out on a cattle ranch, so I keep plenty of the canned stuff on hand. Often a cowboy will eat two cans at once when he comes in from a ride very hungry."

So the six little Bunkers had something to eat, even if it was not supper time, and then they went with Captain Roy to look at the ponies again.

"Oh, look how they run to the fence to meet us!" cried Rose, as some of the ponies in the corral trotted toward the captain and the children.

"That's because they think I have a bit of bread and sugar for them," said Captain Roy.

"Have you?" asked Violet.

"Yes. I hardly ever come out without bringing them something," answered the old soldier.

He reached over the fence to pat the glossy necks and soft noses of the ponies, feeding them bits of dried bread, of which he seemed to have a lot in his pockets.

"Bill Johnson saves me all his old crusts for the ponies," Captain Roy said to Russ. "And if you bring the little horses something to eat each time you come out they'll like you all the more, and get very tame."

"I'll do it," said Russ.

They stood looking at the ponies for some little time, and then Russ decided he wanted to make a boat and sail it in the creek that was not far from the ranch house.

"I'll sail one, too," said Laddie.

"And we'll take our dolls down by the creek and let them have a bath," said Rose to Violet.

"You don't mean a real bath?"

"No, just make believe."

"All right. Only I think I'll make a boat. Su-San doesn't need a bath. She had one once when we were at home. But I'll take her along so she can see the water."

"We'll all go down to the bank of the creek and sit there in the shade until Daddy and Uncle Fred come back," said Mrs. Bunker. "That will make the time pass more quickly."

"I hope they bring back the lost cattle," said Rose.

A little later the six little Bunkers were walking with their mother down toward where a creek flowed through the Three Star Ranch. It was not a very large one, but it had enough water in it to give hundreds of cattle a drink when they were thirsty. When the spring went dry the water from the creek had to be used in the ranch house. But, as Uncle Fred had told the children, there was a tank full of spring water that might last until the dry spell had passed.

Russ and Laddie and Vi—Vi keeping Su-San near by—made some boats out of old pieces of wood they picked up around the ranch house. These boats they tied strings to, and let float down the creek, pulling them back from time to time and starting them off on another voyage.

Mrs. Bunker sat on the grassy bank, in the shade of a willow tree, while Mun Bun and Margy and Rose played near her.

Mun Bun had his pail and shovel that he had brought from the beach at Cousin Tom's, and the little boy began digging holes in the dirt near the edge of the creek. Margy played with her Japanese doll as did Rose.

It was rather warm, for that time of year, and Mrs. Bunker, leaning up against the tree trunk, began to feel sleepy. She closed her eyes, meaning only to rest them a minute, but, before she knew it, she was asleep. The children did not notice her as they were playing so nicely, Russ and Laddie and Vi a little way down the creek, and the other three near their mother.

After a while Margy said:

"I'm going to take a walk with my doll. She hasn't had a

walk to-day."

"Where are you going?" asked Rose.

"Oh, just a little way," Margy answered. "Want to come?"

"No, my doll doesn't feel very well, and I've sent for the doctor. I've got to stay in till he comes," replied Rose.

Of course this was only make-believe, but the children often played that.

She made a bed for her doll in the soft grass, and covered her with some leaves picked near by.

"I guess I'll play my doll is sick, too," said Margy, "'stead of taking her for a walk."

"No, don't play your doll's sick," objected Rose to Margy. "She must be a trained nurse for my doll."

"Oh, yes. That'll be more fun. I wish the doctor would hurry up and come."

"So do I," murmured Rose, pretending to be anxious.

Then, after a while, they made believe the doctor had arrived in his automobile, and he left some medicine for Rose's sick doll, which the trained nurse, who was Margy's doll, had to give with a spoon. The spoon was just a little willow twig, of course.

Down by the creek Russ and Laddie and Vi were still sailing their boats.

Pretty soon Vi said she was tired playing sail-a-boat, and was going to take Su-San for a walk.

After a while Russ and Laddie grew tired of playing boats, and came up the bank to where their mother was.

"Oh, look! She's asleep!" whispered Russ.

"Don't wake her," replied Rose.

But just then Mrs. Bunker opened her eyes and smiled at the children.

"I was asleep," she said, "but I heard what you said. Did you have a nice time? Shall we go back now? It must be almost supper time. Why, where's Vi?" she suddenly asked, as she did not see the curly-haired girl. "Where's Violet?" and Mrs. Bunker stood up quickly and looked all around.

# CHAPTER XII

## LADDIE CATCHES A RIDDLE

Mrs. Bunker was startled when she did not see Violet with the other little Bunkers.

"Where's Vi?" she asked the other children. "Where did she go?"

"Oh, she just took her doll for a walk," said Russ. "She went away a little while ago, over there," and he pointed to the rolling plains behind the willow trees.

The plain was not flat, like a board. It was rolling land, with hills and hollows here and there. Some of the hills were high enough to hide a man behind them.

"Where did she go?" asked Mrs. Bunker, and now her voice was anxious.

"Just to give her doll a walk," explained Russ. "She got tired of playing sail-a-boat, she said, and she went for a walk, and took her doll."

"Violet! Violet! Where are you?" loudly called Mrs. Bunker.

There was no answer.

Mrs. Bunker ran to the top of the nearest little hill, or knoll, and looked across the plain. The five little Bunkers followed her. There were only five with her, as Violet had gone for a walk with her doll.

"But where can she have gone?" asked Mrs. Bunker, as she did not see her little girl, nor hear her answer the call.

"Maybe she went home," said Russ.

"Oh, yes," agreed Rose, not wanting to think that anything had happened to her sister. "Maybe her doll got tired, and she took her home."

Sometimes the little Bunker girls were so real in their make-believe play that they did things a grown person would have done.

"Would she know the way home alone?" asked Mrs. Bunker.

"It's right over there," said Russ, pointing. "You can see the ranch houses from here."

This was true enough. When they were up on the little hill they could see the buildings on Three Star Ranch.

"If she only went that way she will be all right," said Mother Bunker. "But if she walked the other way—"

"Come on! We'll find her!" called Russ to Laddie.

"All right. Wait till I go back and anchor my ship and I'll come."

"No, you mustn't go!" exclaimed Mother Bunker. "We must all keep together. I don't want any more of you getting lost."

"Is Vi lost, Mother?" asked Rose, and she moved over closer to Mrs. Bunker.

"Well, I don't know that she is lost," was the answer. "Probably not. But she isn't here with us. She has wandered away. I'll call again.

"Vi! Violet, where are you?" called Mrs. Bunker, as loudly as she could. But there was no answer. Only the wind rustled the branches of the willow tree and the tall grass near the creek.

"Maybe she fell asleep, same as you did," suggested Laddie to his mother.

"Well, perhaps she did, and if she were to lie down in the tall grass we couldn't see her," said Mrs. Bunker. "Oh, dear! I wish I hadn't gone to sleep, and that Vi hadn't wandered off."

She called again, but there was no answer.

"We'd better go for Daddy!" exclaimed Russ. Daddy Bunker was the one always wanted when anything happened.

"But we can't get him," said Mrs. Bunker. "He has gone away with Uncle Fred to look for the lost cattle."

"Then we'll go for Captain Roy!" went on Russ. "He used to be a soldier, and he'll know how to find lost people."

"Yes, I guess that's the best thing to do," said Mrs. Bunker. "Though I hate to go away and leave Violet all alone here, wherever she is. But it's the only way to find her. Come, we'll hurry back to the house and get Captain Roy."

So the five little Bunkers and their mother hurried over the plain toward the Three Star Ranch house.

And now I know you are wondering what happened to Violet, so I am going to tell you. For you know a book-writer can be in two places at the same time.

When Violet started out to give her doll a walk the little girl had no notion of going very far. If she had been at home she would have gone just down to the corner of her block and back. But there are no corners or blocks on the open plain, so Violet just walked over the green fields.

"Do you like it here, Su-San?" she asked.

"Oh, you do," she went on, pretending that her doll had spoken. "And you want to go a little farther, don't you?"

Violet made believe listen to what her doll said.

"Oh, you want to pick some flowers. Well, that will be nice," went on the little girl. "We'll pick a nice bouquet and we'll take it to Rose's doll."

There were flowers growing on the plain, and Violet began picking some, making believe her doll helped. Now, you know how it is when you go to pick blossoms. First you see a nice one, then, farther on, you see one that is a little better, and pretty soon you see one that is prettier than all, and you go for that one, and, before you know it, you are a long way from where you started.

That is what happened to Violet. She wandered on and on, down among the little hills and hollows until she was quite a distance from the willow tree and the creek. She could no longer see the tree.

And Violet forgot, or she did not know, that when one is in a big field, down among the hills and hollows, and can't see anything high and tall, like a tree or a building sticking up, that one doesn't know which way to go. All ways look alike then. So it is no wonder that Vi, after she had helped her doll gather a bouquet, went the wrong way. Instead of walking back toward the creek she walked away from it.

And she was walking away from the Three Star Ranch house also. In fact Violet was lost on the plain, and she was getting more and more lost every minute and with each step she took.

Finally she said:

"Oh, Su-San! aren't you tired? I am. I'm going to sit down and rest and let you rest, too."

Of course the doll wasn't tired, as she hadn't done any walking, for Vi had carried her all the way. But Vi pretended that the doll was as weary as was the little girl herself.

So together they sat down in the tall grass, which came over Violet's head now, and rested. Violet didn't know she was lost. But she was, all the same.

After a while she got up and started to walk again. She walked and walked, and, when she couldn't find the creek nor the willow tree nor see her mother nor any of the other little Bunkers, she became frightened and started to cry.

"Oh, Mother!" she called, "where are you? I want you!"

Of course Mrs. Bunker could not hear then, for she was on her way to get Captain Roy to help search for the little girl.

Violet wandered around and around, calling now and then, and crying real tears every once in a while, until, at last, when the sun began to get lower and lower in the west, and the little girl knew it would soon be dark, she sobbed:

"Oh, what shall I do! Oh, where is my mother!"

And just then she heard a horse come trotting along. She could hear the gallop of the hoofs on the ground.

"Oh, maybe it's an Indian!" thought Vi. "We'd better hide, Su-San!"

She clasped the Japanese toy in her arms, and crouched down in the grass. But the trotting came nearer. Then Violet knew it was more than one horse.

"Maybe it's a whole band of Indians!" she whispered. "Oh, Su-San!"

Down in the tall grass she hid, but she kept on crying. And then, suddenly, close to her, a voice said:

"I thought I heard a child crying just now, didn't you, Jim?"

"Sounded like it, but what would a child be doing out here all alone?"

"I don't know, but I sure did hear it!"

Then another voice called:

"What's the matter over there?"

"Oh, Frank thought he heard a child crying," answered some one, and Vi thought it didn't sound like an Indian.

"A child!" cried still another voice. "Oh, I wonder—"

Then Violet didn't hear any more, for standing right over where she crouched in the grass was a big man on a big horse and he was looking right down on her.

"I've found her!" the man cried. "It's one of the six little Bunkers!"

"One of the six little Bunkers!" repeated a voice that Violet well knew. It was her father's.

"Oh, Daddy! Daddy!" she cried. "Here I am! I got lost, and I can't find the creek, nor the willow tree, nor Mother, nor anything. Here I am!"

Violet stood up, and a moment later, her father had ridden his horse over to where she was and, reaching down, took her and the doll up in his arms.

"Well, how in the world did you get here?" he asked in surprise. "Where have you been, Violet?"

Then Violet told, and Uncle Fred, who was with Daddy Bunker and some of the cowboys, said:

"We'd better ride back to the house as fast as we can. Amy is probably wild now about losing her. Hurry back to the house!"

Then how the horses did gallop! And Vi, sitting in front of Daddy on his saddle, had a fine ride and forgot she had been lost.

They got back to the house just as Captain Roy and some cowboys were about to ride away in search of Violet. For Mrs. Bunker and the other little Bunkers had reached the ranch house with the story of the lost one.

"How did you find her?" asked Mrs. Bunker of her husband when Violet had been hugged and kissed.

"We were riding back," said Daddy Bunker, "when one of the cowboys heard a child crying. He found Violet in the grass, and then I took her up. How did she get lost?"

Then Mrs. Bunker told about the trip to the creek and how Vi had wandered away by herself.

"But I'm never going again," said the little girl. "I thought the Indians were after me!"

"And it was only Daddy Bunker!" laughed her father.

"Did you find the lost cattle?" asked his wife, when supper was over and they had ceased talking about Vi being lost.

"No, the men who took them must have hurried away with them. We could not find them at all."

Just as the six little Bunkers were going to bed a cowboy came up to the ranch house to say that the water was coming back into the spring.

"That's good," said Uncle Fred. "But I certainly would like to know what makes it go out, and who takes our cattle."

The next day Russ and Laddie asked if they could go fishing in the creek, if they went to one place and stayed there, so they might not wander away and be lost.

"Yes, I guess so," returned Daddy Bunker. "It isn't far, and if you stay on shore you won't fall in."

"True," chuckled Uncle Fred, but he wouldn't tell Laddie what he was laughing at.

There were some small fish to be caught in the creek, and soon, with hooks, lines, poles and bait Russ and Laddie started for the creek.

"I hope they'll be all right," said their mother.

They had been gone about an hour when Russ came running back to the house, dragging his pole after him, and on the line was a fish, which he had not stopped to take off.

"Oh, Mother! Daddy!" cried Russ. "Laddie—Laddie—"

"Has he fallen in?" cried Mrs. Bunker.

"No, Mother! It isn't that!" said Russ. "But he's caught a riddle, and he doesn't know what to do with it."

"He's caught a *riddle*?" cried Uncle Fred. "What do you mean?"

"Well, he found it, or caught it, I don't know which," said Russ.

"How did he catch a riddle?" asked Daddy Bunker.

"On his hook. It's a funny thing, like a black stone, and it wiggles and sticks its head out, and Laddie doesn't know what it is, and when you don't know what a thing is that's a riddle, isn't it? Come and see!"

And down to the creek went Daddy and Mother Bunker to see the riddle that Laddie had caught.

# CHAPTER XIII

## ON THE PONIES

Mr. and Mrs. Bunker found Laddie sitting on the bank of the creek looking at something on the ground near him.

"What is it?" called Daddy Bunker, as Russ led them up to the place where he and his brother had been fishing. "What have you caught?"

"I—I guess it's a riddle, for I don't know what else it is," answered Laddie. "Come and look."

"Better not touch it," cautioned his mother.

"I'm not going to touch it, 'cause it can bite. It's got a funny head and a mouth," said Laddie, "and it bit on my hook and it's got it yet."

Mr. and Mrs. Bunker hurried over and saw what Laddie had caught. As Russ had said, it was rough, like a stone, and as black and hard-looking as a rock. But it was alive and moved.

"Why, it's a mud turtle!" exclaimed Daddy Bunker, as he took a good look at the creature. "It's nothing but a mud

Laura Lee Hope

turtle, Laddie! I should think you'd know what they are, for you have seen them in Rainbow River at home."

"No, this isn't a mud turtle," said Russ. "I know what a mud turtle is, and this is different. It's something like one, but not the same."

"How did you get it, Laddie?" asked Mother Bunker.

"Well, I was fishing, and I got a lot of nibbles but none of the fish stayed on my hook. Then, all of a sudden, this one stayed on, and I pulled him up, only it isn't a fish."

"I should say not!" exclaimed another voice, and they looked up to see Uncle Fred standing near them. He had followed Daddy and Mother Bunker to the place where the boys were fishing.

"What is it?" asked Russ.

"That's a snapping turtle—not a mud turtle," went on the ranchman. "They're very hard biters, and if a big one gets hold of your finger or toe he might bite it off, or at least hurt it very much. So keep away from these fellows."

"I thought it didn't look like a mud turtle," said Russ.

"It is something like one, but different in shape," went on Uncle Fred. "We'll just cut this one off your line, Laddie."

The line was cut, and the turtle, that had the hook in its mouth, crawled down toward the creek. It had tried to crawl away before, but could not because the fishing line held it.

"They get their mouth closed tight, and don't like to open their jaws," said Uncle Fred, as the turtle disappeared under the water with a splash. "But I guess this one will open his mouth and let go the hook when he gets off by himself. This is the largest snapper I've seen around here. The Indians say they're good to eat, but I've never tried it."

"Well, I did catch something like a riddle, didn't I?" asked Laddie.

"Yes. And Uncle Fred guessed the riddle," answered Russ. "Now we'll fish some more."

"And I don't want to catch any more snappers," said Laddie, when Uncle Fred had fastened a new hook on his line.

The grown folk went back to the ranch house, leaving the boys to fish, and, somewhat to their own surprise, Laddie and Russ each caught two good-sized fish.

With shouts of delight, about an hour after having captured the snapping turtle, they ran to the house, holding up on strings the prizes they had caught.

"We'll have 'em cooked!" cried Laddie. "They're good to eat! One of the cowboys told us they were."

"Yes, those fish are good to eat," said Uncle Fred. "I'll have Bill Johnson clean and cook them for you."

"This is better than riddles!" laughed Russ. "I'm going fishing every day and catch fish."

"And I'm going, too," declared Violet.

"Good!" cried her father. "Then Uncle Fred won't have to buy so many things at the store."

Laura Lee Hope

The fish were cooked, and very good they were, too, though Mun Bun said they had too many bones in them, and this, perhaps, was true. But all fish have bones.

As the days went on Uncle Fred and his men, as well as Daddy Bunker, tried to find the lost cattle, or the men who, it was thought, had taken them. But they could not. The cattle seemed to have vanished, leaving no trace.

Every day some of the six little Bunkers, and, sometimes, all of them, went to the mysterious spring, to see if any of the water had run out, but it seemed to be all right, and behaving just as a spring should.

"Though there's no telling when it will go dry again," said Uncle Fred. "We'll have to keep watch of it. For nearly every time the spring goes dry I lose some cattle."

"May we go for a ride on our ponies to-day?" asked Russ of his mother one morning. "Laddie and I want a ride."

"Will you be very careful," asked his mother, "not to go outside the big field?"

"Oh, yes, we'll just stay in the big field," promised Laddie. "Come on, Russ! We'll have some fun!"

The four older Bunker children had learned to ride the little Shetland ponies very well. Uncle Fred had let them take, for their own use, four of the best animals, which were kind and gentle. He had also set aside for them a big fenced-in field, where they might ride.

Over to the corral Russ and Laddie ran, and soon they were leading out their own two special ponies. A little later they were riding them around the big fenced-in meadow, playing they were cowboys and Indians, though Russ was not allowed to have a lasso. Uncle Fred had said that if a little boy, like Russ, played with a rope while riding a pony, the cord might get tangled in the pony's legs, and throw it.

"This is lots of fun!" cried Laddie, as he trotted about.

"Most fun we ever had!" agreed Russ.

But as the six little Bunkers said this every place they went, you can take it for what it is worth. Certainly they were having good times at Uncle Fred's.

When Russ and Laddie were giving their ponies a rest in the shade of a tree that grew at one side of the field, they heard a voice calling to them:

"Give me a ride! Oh, please give me a ride!"

"It's Margy!" cried Russ, looking around. "How'd you get here, Margy?" he asked.

"I walked," stated the little girl. "Mother and Daddy have gone to the store with Violet to get her a new dress, and Mun Bun has gone, too. I stayed at home with Rose."

"Where is Rose now?" asked Laddie.

"She is out in the kitchen, making a pie. Bill Johnson said she could. So I took a walk to come over to see you, and I want a ride."

"Shall we give her a ride?" asked Laddie.

"I'd like to," Russ answered. "But how can we? Mother said we couldn't take any one on the same pony with us, 'cause we couldn't hold 'em on tight enough."

"If we only had a little cart we could give her a ride," said Laddie. "We could sit on our pony's back and one of us could pull her in the cart. But we haven't got a cart."

"Please, I want a ride!" repeated Margy.

Russ didn't say anything for a moment. Then he suddenly exclaimed:

"I know how we can give her a ride!"

"How?" asked Laddie. "Can you make a cart?"

"No, but I can make something just as good!" exclaimed Russ, and he began whistling. "You wait, Margy! I'll give you a ride!"

Russ tied his pony to the fence and hurried over toward the barn, telling Margy to crawl in under the fence and wait until he came back.

Margy was going to have a ride, and there was to be a queer ending to it.

# CHAPTER XIV

## MUN BUN'S PIE

Russ Bunker came back from the barn, dragging with him some long bean poles, an old bag that had held oats for the horses, and some pieces of rope.

"Are you going to make a swing?" asked Margy.

"I'm going to make something for you to ride in," answered Russ.

"A carriage?" asked Laddie.

"An Indian carriage," Russ answered. "One of the cowboys was telling me about 'em. The Indians fasten two poles, one on each side of a horse. Then they tie the ends of the poles that drag on the ground together with some ropes, and they stick a bag or a piece of cloth between the poles, and tie it there.

"That makes a place where you can sit or lie down, or put something you want to carry. And that's where we'll put Margy."

"Oh, I'll like a ride like that!" exclaimed the little girl. "I was in the kitchen with Rose, but I came out 'cause she's making a pie. I'll go back when the pie is done, and get a piece."

"So'll I," added Laddie with a laugh. "I like pie!"

He and Russ began to make the queer carriage in which Margy was to ride. Perhaps you may have seen them in Indian pictures. A long pole is fastened on either side of a horse, being tied to the edge of the saddle. The ends drag behind the horse on the ground, and between these poles is a platform, or a piece of bagging stretched, in which the Indian squaws and their papooses, or babies, ride. It is just like a carriage or cart, except that it has no wheels.

It took Russ and Laddie longer than they thought it would to make the Indian carriage for Margy. But at last it was finished, and there, dragging behind Russ's pony, were the two long poles, and a bag was tied between them for Margy to sit on.

"All aboard!" cried Laddie, when it was finished.

"Hey! This isn't a ship! You don't say all aboard!" exclaimed Russ.

"What do you say?"

"Well, you say get in, or something like that. Not 'all aboard!' That's only for boats or maybe trains."

"Well, get in, Margy," said Laddie. "Russ will ride ahead and pull you, and I'll ride behind, just as if I was another Indian. That's what we'll play—Indian!" he said.

"All right," agreed Russ.

"Oh, this is fun!" exclaimed Margy, when she was seated in the Indian carriage and Russ's pony was pulling her about the field. "I like it."

Indeed she was having a nice ride, though it was rather bumpy when the dragging poles went over stones or holes in the ground. But Margy did not mind that, for the bag seat in which she was cuddled was nice and soft.

Once one of the poles, which were fastened to the pony with pieces of clothesline, came loose, and the pony walked around dragging only one, so that Margy was spilled out. But the grass was soft, and she only laughed at the accident.

Russ tied the pole back again, and then he and Laddie rode around the field, Margy being dragged after them, just as, in the olden days, the real Indians used to give their squaws and papooses a ride from one part of the country to another.

"I guess the ponies are tired now," said Laddie, as he noticed his walking rather slowly. "Maybe we'd better give them a rest."

"I guess so," agreed Russ. "We'll let 'em rest in the shade of the tree."

So they rode their ponies into the shade and left them standing there, the boys themselves running around in the grass, to "stretch their legs," as their father used to call it.

"Margy's asleep," said Russ, as he got down from his pony and saw that his little sister's eyes were closed, as she lay cuddled up in the bag between the two trailing poles. "We'll let her sleep while we play tag."

And so Margy slept in the Indian carriage, while Russ and

Laddie raced about the big field. Then they forgot all about Margy, for they heard Rose calling to them:

"Russ! Laddie! Do you want some of my pie? I baked it all myself in Bill Johnson's oven!"

"Oh, her pie is done!" cried Laddie.

"Come on! Let's get some!" added Russ.

Then the two boys, forgetting all about Margy sleeping in the Indian carriage, ran out of the field, leaving the ponies behind them, and leaving their little sister also.

"Is it a real pie?" asked Russ, as he reached the ranch house, in front of which stood Rose.

"Course it is," she answered.

"And has it got a crust, and things inside, like Norah makes?" Laddie wanted to know.

"Course it has," declared Rose. "Come on, I'll give you some."

They went out to the kitchen where Bill Johnson was busy. He greeted the boys with a laugh.

"That little sister of yours is some cook!" exclaimed the cook. "She can make a pie almost as good as I can, and it took me a good many years to learn."

"Let's see the pie!" demanded Russ.

"Here 'tis!" exclaimed Rose. "We set it out on the window sill to cool," and she brought in what seemed like a very nice pie, indeed.

And it was good, too, as the boys said after they had tasted it. True, it was made of canned peaches, but then you can't get fresh peaches on a Western ranch in early summer. Canned ones did very well.

"Could I have another piece?" asked Laddie, finishing his first.

"Well, a little one," said Rose. "I want to save some for Margy—Oh, where is Margy?" she suddenly cried. "I forgot all about her, and Mother said I was to watch her! Oh, where is she?"

Rose started up in alarm, but Laddie said:

"Margy is all right. She came over where me and Russ—I mean, Russ and I—were riding our ponies, and we made an Indian carriage for her," and he explained what they had done.

"But where is she now?" Rose demanded.

"She's asleep over there," Russ said slowly, and pointed to the big field.

"Let's go and get her, and we'll take her this piece of pie," proposed Laddie. "If she doesn't want it I'll eat it."

"No, I will!" cried Russ. "You've had two pieces."

"Margy will want it all right!" declared Rose. "She likes pie. I'm going to make another some day."

Carrying Margy's piece of pie, the three little Bunkers went over to the field where the ponies had been left. On the way Russ told Rose more about the queer Indian carriage he had made.

"Will it hold me?" Rose asked.

"Yes, and I'll give you a ride after Margy wakes up," Russ promised. "I'll get some more poles for Laddie's pony and he can ride Vi and I'll ride you."

"Oh, won't that be fun!" cried Rose.

But when they reached the field where the ponies had been left a sad surprise awaited them. Neither of the two little creatures were to be seen, and there was no sign of Margy or the queer Indian carriage either.

"Oh, they—they're gone!" gasped Russ.

"Both ponies!" added Laddie.

"And where's Margy?" asked Rose, holding the piece of pie in her hand.

"She's gone, too," said Russ. "Oh, dear!"

"Maybe the Indians came and took her," said Laddie.

"I don't see any Indians," and Russ shook his head.

"But maybe they rode off with her."

"Or maybe the bad men that took Uncle Fred's cattle came and took the ponies and Margy," said Rose. "Oh, what are we going to do?"

"We must tell Uncle Fred!" exclaimed Russ.

"He's away off at the far end of the ranch," said Rose. "He rode over with some of the cowboys when I was making my pie."

"Is Mother or Daddy back?" asked Laddie.

"No, not yet," Rose answered. "Oh, dear! Mother will say it is my fault, for she told me to watch Margy, but I forgot when I was making my pie."

The pie seemed to give Russ an idea.

"We'll tell Bill Johnson," he said. "Bill used to be a cowboy, if he is a cook now, and he'll know how to find anybody the Indians have taken. We'll go and tell Bill Johnson."

So back to the ranch house rushed the children, bursting in on Bill Johnson with an excited story about the missing ponies and Margy.

"Ponies gone out of the big field, eh?" asked Bill. "Well, I expect you left the bars down, didn't you—the place where you made a hole in the fence to drive the ponies in from the corral? Did you leave the bars down?"

"I guess we did," admitted Russ.

"Come on with me," said Bill with a laugh. "I guess I can find the ponies for you."

"But we want Margy, too!" said Rose.

"Yes, I guess I can find her also."

Bill Johnson led the way to the corral, where the ponies were kept, and there, among their fellows, were the two missing ones. And, best of all, the sticks were still fast to the one Russ had ridden, and Margy was just awakening and was still in her place in the bag between the poles.

"Oh, Margy!" cried Rose, "I brought you some pie."

"I had a nice ride," said Margy, and she sat up, rubbing her eyes. "Russ gave me a nice ride, and we played Indian, and I went to sleep."

"Yes, and while you slept," said Bill, "the two ponies took a notion they wanted to go back with the others in the corral. So they just walked through the fence, where the bars were down, and went out, the one dragging Margy with it. It's a good thing you made the Indian carriage so good and strong, Russ, or she might have been hurt. After this don't leave ponies alone in a field with the bars down."

The boys promised they wouldn't. Margy was lifted out, the poles were taken off Russ's pony and the children went back to the ranch house.

Of course, Mrs. Bunker had to caution Russ and Laddie to be a little more careful when she heard the tale.

The six little Bunkers had lots of fun at Uncle Fred's. Each day there was something new to see or do, and as the weather became warmer they were outdoors from morning until night.

One day Margy and Mun Bun went off by themselves with the pails and shovels they had played with at the beach when they visited Cousin Tom.

"Don't go too far," called their mother after them. "Don't go out of sight of the house."

"We won't," they promised.

"I just goin' to make mud pies down by the pond," said Mun Bun.

The "pond" was a place where the creek widened out into a shallow place, only half-way to Mun Bun's knees in depth. On one shore was sand, where "pies" could be made.

It was about half an hour after Mun Bun and Margy had gone to play on the shore of the creek that Margy came running back alone.

"Where's Mun Bun?" her mother asked her.

"He's in a mud pie and he can't get out," explained the little girl. "Come on, and get Mun Bun out of the mud pie."

# CHAPTER XV

## THE WIND WAGON

For a moment Mrs. Bunker did not know whether Margy was fooling or not. She could not imagine how Mun Bun could be stuck in a "mud pie," and yet that was what Margy had said.

"Is he hurt?" asked Mrs. Bunker, as she laid aside her sewing and got ready to follow Margy to the creek.

"No. He's only just stuck in the middle of his big pie, and he can't get out. And he's all mud and he looks awful funny."

"I should think he would!" exclaimed the mother of the six little Bunkers. "Hurry along, Margy, and show me where he is."

"What's the matter now?" asked Daddy Bunker, who came along just then, in time to hear what his wife said. "What has happened to Mun Bun now?"

"He is stuck in a mud pie, so Margy says," answered Mrs. Bunker. "Perhaps you had better come with me and see what it's all about."

Together Mr. and Mrs. Bunker hurried after Margy. As they came within sight of the pond they could not see Mun Bun at all.

"Where is he?" asked the little chap's mother. "Where did you leave him, Margy?"

"There he is—right over there!" answered the little girl. She pointed to something that, at first, did not look at all like Mun Bun. But as Mr. Bunker took a second glance he saw that it was his little boy, and Mun Bun was, indeed, "stuck in a mud pie."

"Why he's in a regular bog-hole!" cried Mr. Bunker. "He must have waded out into the water for something or other, and he got stuck in the mud."

"And he has sunk down!" cried Mrs. Bunker. "Get him out right away, Daddy! He may be smothered in the mud!"

"I'll get him!" cried Mun Bun's father.

Mr. Bunker took off his shoes and socks and, rolling up his trousers so they would not get muddy, waded out to where his little boy was. Truly Mun Bun was stuck in the middle of a big mud pie—at least that was what Margy called it. It was, however, the muddy bottom of the pond itself, which, at one end, was a regular bog, being fenced off so no cattle or horses could get in.

But Mun Bun had climbed in under the fence, and at once he found himself in soft mud. He had begun to sink down; so he called for help, and Margy ran to tell her mother.

"My, but you are a sight, Mun Bun!" cried his father, as he came to the side of the little boy and began pulling him out.

And Mun Bun was stuck so fast in the mud that Mr. Bunker had to pull quite hard to loosen him. And when Mun Bun came up, his legs and feet making a funny, sucking sound as they were pulled out, he was covered with mud and water from his toes to his waist. Mud was splashed up on his face, too, and his hands—well, they didn't look like hands at all! They were just "gobs of mud," Margy said.

"How did it happen? What made you go in the mud?" asked the little boy's mother, as Daddy Bunker waded to shore with Mun Bun.

"Well, I made some mud pies in the sand," Mun Bun explained, "and then I thought maybe if I could find a mud turkle he'd eat the pies. So I crawled under the fence and went in the deep mud to look for a mud turkle."

Mun Bun meant a "turtle," of course.

"But I didn't find any," he went on, "and I went down deeper and deeper, and then I hollered like anything."

"And I heard him," said Margy. "I was going to wade in and get him, but my feet went down deep in the mud, so I ran for you."

"It's a good thing you did," said her mother. "You mustn't come here again. You might get stuck and never get out. Never come here again!"

"Can't we make mud pies in the sand?" asked Mun Bun.

"Yes, but you mustn't hunt for mud turtles. Stay outside the bog fence."

The children promised that they would, and then came the

work of washing Mun Bun and Margy. Margy was the easiest to clean, as she only had mud on her up to her knees. She waded in the creek where there was a clean, sandy bottom, and where the water was clear, and soon the mud was washed off her.

"But as for Mun Bun," said his father, "I guess I'll have to put him in the creek, clothes and all, up to his neck, and let the water wash the mud away."

"I guess you'd better," said Mrs. Bunker. "That's the only way to get off the mud."

The day was warm, and so was the water, so Mun Bun was set down in the creek at a clean place, and he and his clothes were washed at the same time. The mud was rinsed from his hands and face and, in time, it came off his feet, legs and clothes.

"It's just like I been in swimming with all my things on!" laughed Mun Bun, as his father lifted him out of the pond.

"Well, don't make any more mud pies right away," his mother told him, and Mun Bun promised not to.

The other little Bunkers laughed when they heard what had happened to Mun Bun.

"Maybe I could make up a riddle about Mun Bun in a mud pie," said Laddie.

"I don't want you to!" the little boy exclaimed. "I don't want to be in a riddle."

"All right. Then I'll make up one about something else," went on Laddie. "This is it. What is it you cannot take from the top of a house to the bottom?"

"Pooh! that isn't a riddle," said Russ.

"Say it again," begged Rose.

"What is it you can't take from the top of a house and put it on the bottom—I mean like down cellar?" asked Laddie.

"There isn't anything," declared Violet. "If you got anything in the top of your house you can take it down cellar, if you want to; can't you, Daddy?"

"Well, I should think so, yes," answered Mr. Bunker.

"No, you can't!" declared Laddie. "Do you all give up? What is it in the top of the house that you can't take down cellar with you?"

"The chimney," answered Russ.

"Nope," said Laddie. "'Cause the chimney starts down cellar, anyhow, and goes up to the top. I mean what's in the top of a house you can't take down cellar?"

"We'll give up," said his mother. "What is it?"

"A hole in the roof!" answered Laddie with a laugh. "You can't take a hole in the roof down cellar, can you?"

"No, I guess you can't," admitted Uncle Fred. "That's a pretty good riddle, Laddie."

It was two or three days after Mun Bun had become stuck in the mud pie that the children awakened one morning to find a high wind blowing outside.

"Oh, is this a cyclone?" asked Violet, for she had heard they had such winds in the West.

"Oh, no, this wind is nothing like as strong as a cyclone," answered Uncle Fred. "It's just one of our summer winds. They're strong, but they do no damage. Look out for your hair if you go outdoors; it might blow off."

"My hair can't blow off 'cause it's fast to me—it's growed fast!" explained Violet.

"Well, then be careful it doesn't blow you away, hair and all!" said Uncle Fred, but by the way he laughed Violet knew he was only joking.

The children went out to play, and they had to hold their hats on most of the time, as the wind blew across the plain so strongly. But the six little Bunkers did not mind.

"If we only had a boat, and the pond was big enough, we could have a fine sail!" cried Laddie, as he looked at the wind making little waves on the place where Mun Bun had been stuck in the mud.

"Oh, I know what we could make!" suddenly exclaimed Russ.

"What?" his brother wanted to know.

"A wind wagon."

"A wind wagon?"

"Yes, you know, a wagon that the wind will blow. Come on, we'll do it. Mother read me a story once about a boy who lived in the West, and he made himself a wind wagon and he had a nice ride. Come on, we'll make one!"

Laura Lee Hope

# CHAPTER XVI

## "CAPTAIN RUSS"

Laddie knew Russ could make many play-things, for he had seen his brother at work. But a wind wagon was something new. Laddie did not see how this could be made.

"Where are you going to get your wagon?" he asked Russ, as the two boys went out to the barn.

"There's an old express wagon out here. I saw it the other day. It's broken, but maybe we can fix it. Uncle Fred said it belonged to a family that used to live on this ranch before he bought it. We'll make the wind wagon out of that."

In a corner of the barn, under a pile of trash and rubbish, was found an old, broken toy express wagon.

"The four wheels are all right, and that's the main thing," said Russ. "We can fix the other part. The wheels you must have, else you can't make a wind wagon. Come on! We'll have lots of fun."

Then began the making of the wind wagon, though Laddie, even yet, didn't know exactly what Russ meant by it. But Russ soon told his brother what he was going to do, and not only told him, but showed him.

"You see, Laddie," explained Russ, "a water ship sails on the ocean or a lake 'cause the wind blows on the sail and makes it go."

"Yes," answered Laddie, "I know that."

"Well, 'stead of a water ship, I'm going to make a wind ship that will go on land. I'll fix the old express wagon up so it will roll along on wheels."

"Do you mean to have a pony pull it?"

"No. Though we could do it that way, if we wanted to. And maybe we will if the wind wagon won't work. But I think it will. You see, we'll fasten a sail to the wagon, and then we'll get in it and the wind will blow on the sail and blow us along as fast as anything."

"It'll be lots of fun!" exclaimed Laddie.

Russ and Laddie so often made things, or, at least, tried to do so, that their father and mother never paid much attention to the boys when they heard them hammering, sawing or battering away, with Russ whistling one merry tune after another. He always whistled when he made things. And now he was going to make a wind wagon.

It was not as easy as the boys had thought it would be to get the broken express wagon so it would run. The wheels were rusty on the axles, and they squeaked when Russ tried to turn them.

"And they've got to run easy if we want to ride," he said.

However, one of the cowboys saw that the boys were making something, and when they told him the trouble with the rusty wheels he gave them some axle grease that he used on the big wagons. After that the wheels spun around easily.

"Now we'll go fast!" cried Russ.

With a hammer and some nails, which he and Laddie found in the barn, they nailed the broken express wagon together, for some of the bottom boards were loose, as well as one of the sides.

But at last, after an hour of hard work, the wagon was in pretty good shape. It could be pulled about, and it would hold the two boys.

"Now we have to make a mast for the sail," said Russ, "and we must get a piece of cloth for the sail, and we've got to have some way to guide the wagon."

"Couldn't I stick my foot out back, and steer that way, same as I do when I'm coasting downhill in winter?" asked Laddie.

"Nope," Russ answered. "We'll have to steer by the front wheels, same as an automobile steers. But I can tie a rope to the front wheels, and pull it whichever way I want to go, just like Jimmie Brackson used to steer his coaster wagon down the hill at home."

He tied a rope on the front axle, close to each front wheel, and then, by pulling on the cords, he could turn the wagon whichever way he wanted to make it go.

"The mast is going to be hard," said Russ, and he and Laddie found it so. They could not make it stand upright, and at last they had to call on Daddy Bunker.

"Oh, so you're going to make a ship to sail on dry land, are you?" asked their father, when they told him their troubles with the mast.

"Will it sail?" asked Laddie.

"Well, it may, a little way. The wind is very strong to-day. I'll help you fix it."

With Daddy Bunker's aid, the mast was soon fixed so that it stood straight up in front of the wagon, being nailed fast and braced. Then they found some pieces of old bags for sails, and these were sewed together and made fast to the mast. There was a gaff, which is the little slanting stick at the top of a sail, and a boom, which is the big stick at the bottom. Only the whole sail, gaff, boom and all, was not very large.

"If you have your sail too big," said Daddy Bunker, "it will tip your wagon over when the wind blows hard. Better have a smaller sail and go a bit slower, than have an accident."

At last the sail was finished and hoisted on the mast. Russ and Laddie took their places in the wagon, and Daddy Bunker turned it around so the wind would blow straight from the back. The wagon stood on a smooth part of the prairies, where the grass had been eaten short by the hundreds of Uncle Fred's cattle.

"All ready, boys?" called their father to them.

"All ready!" answered Russ.

"All aboard!" answered Laddie. "I can say that this time, 'cause this is really a ship, though it sails on dry land," he added.

Laura Lee Hope

"Yes, you can say that," agreed Russ.

"Here you go!" cried Daddy Bunker.

He gave the wind wagon a shove, and it began to move. Slowly it went at first, and then, as the wind struck the sail, it began to send the toy along faster.

"Hurray!" cried Russ. "We're sailing!"

"Fine!" shouted Laddie.

And the boys were really moving over the level prairie in the wind wagon Russ had made. They could only go straight, or nearly so, and could not sail much to one side or the other, as their land ship was not like a water one. It would not "tack," or move across the wind.

Along they sailed, rather bumpily, it is true, but Russ and Laddie did not mind that. Russ could pull on the ropes fast to the front wheels, and steer his "ship" out of the way of stones and holes.

"Well, the youngsters did pretty well!" exclaimed Uncle Fred, as he saw Russ and Laddie sailing along.

"Yes, they did better than I expected they would," said their father. "If they don't upset they'll be all right."

Laddie and Russ did not seem to be going to do this. The wind wagon appeared to be a great success.

"Oh, who made it? Where did you get it? Whose is it? Can't I have a ride?" cried Violet, when she saw the new toy.

"My, what a lot of questions!" exclaimed Daddy

Bunker, laughing.

"We'll give everybody a ride," said Russ, "only I'm going to sit in the ship each time and steer. I'm the captain, and nobody knows how to steer except me."

When Laddie got out, Rose had a turn, and then Violet was given a ride. The wind wagon went very nicely. Of course, each time it was blown over the field, some distance from the ranch house, it had to be dragged back again, as the children did not want to ride too far from home.

But walking back with the land ship to the starting point was no worse than walking back uphill with a sled, as the children had to do when they went coasting in the winter.

"And we walk back on level ground, not up a hill," said Russ.

So the wind wagon was that much better than a sled.

It came the turns of Mun Bun and Margy, and they liked the rides very much. Only Mun Bun made trouble by wanting to guide the land ship, and when he was told he could not, he snatched at the ropes Russ held, and nearly made the wind wagon upset.

After that Mun Bun was not given any more rides.

"I guess he is cross because he hasn't had his sleep this afternoon," said his mother. "Come on, Margy and Mun Bun. I'll put you to bed."

So Russ, with Laddie, Violet and Rose, played with the wind wagon after the two smallest Bunkers had been put to bed.

But Russ began to feel that he had been a little selfish, and each of the older children was allowed to guide the land ship some of the time.

The wind kept blowing harder and harder, and at last the land ship went so fast before the breeze that Mr. Bunker called:

"Better shorten sail, Russ! Better take in some, or you may blow over."

"Oh, I don't guess we will," said Russ, who was again, as he was most of the time, doing the guiding.

But he did not know what was going to happen.

"The wind is blowing so strong now," said Laddie to his brother, "that three of us could ride in the wagon 'stead of only two. It will blow three of us."

"We'll try it," agreed Russ. "Come on, Vi and Rose. I'll give you two a ride at the same time."

It was rather a tight squeeze to get the three children in the wagon, but it was managed. Laddie shoved them off and away they went.

The wind blew harder and harder, and, all of a sudden, as Russ steered out of the way of a stone, there came a sudden puff, and—over went the wind wagon, spilling out Rose, Violet and "Captain Russ" himself. The mast broke off close to where it was fastened to the toy wagon, and the sail became tangled in the arms and legs of the children.

"My goodness!" cried Captain Roy, who came along just in time to see the accident, which happened a little way from the ranch house. "Any of the six little Bunkers hurt?"

"There's only three of us in the wagon," said Russ, as he crawled out. "I'm not hurt. Are you, Rose?"

"No," she answered, laughing. "But where's Vi?"

"Here I am," answered the little girl, as she crawled out from under the wagon, which had upset. "And I don't like that way of stopping at all, Russ Bunker! I like to stop easy!"

"So do I," said Russ. "I didn't mean to do that. The wind was too strong for us. Now the wagon is busted."

It was indeed broken, and, as the wind blew harder than before, Daddy Bunker said it would not be best to use the wind wagon any more, even if it had not been smashed. So the toy was turned right side up, the broken mast and sail put in it and Russ and Laddie took it to the barn.

"We'll fix it up again to-morrow," said Russ.

The children had other fun the rest of that day, and in the evening they all had pony rides. And this time Margy was not given a ride in the Indian carriage and left asleep. She had her own pony to ride on.

The next day, when dinner was about to be served, Uncle Fred came in looking rather thoughtful.

"Has anything happened?" asked Mother Bunker.

"Yes," he answered. "Some more of my cattle have been taken. I thought this would happen after the spring started to go dry. I wish I could find out what it all means—why the water runs out of the spring, and who is taking my cattle."

Laura Lee Hope

"I wish we could help," said Daddy Bunker. "But we don't seem able to. The engineers you asked about it don't seem to know what makes your spring go dry; the books tell nothing about it, and we can't find any of your lost cattle. I'm afraid we Bunkers aren't helping any."

"Well, I like to have you here!" said Uncle Fred. "Three Star Ranch would be lonesome if the six little Bunkers went away. Just stay on, and maybe we'll solve the riddle yet."

They were just going in to dinner, when a cowboy rode up on a pony that was covered with foam, from having been ridden far and fast.

"What's the matter?" asked Uncle Fred, as he went out to talk to the man—for cowboys are men, though they are called boys. "Are any more of my cattle gone?"

"No, but they're likely to be. There's a big prairie fire started some miles south of here, and the wind is blowing it right this way. We've got to do something if we want to save the ranch houses from burning!"

# CHAPTER XVII

## A CATTLE STAMPEDE

"What's that?" cried Uncle Fred. "A prairie fire?"

"Yes, and a bad one, too," answered the man. "I saw it when I was bringing in those steers you told me to get ready to ship away on the train. I just left them, knowing they'd keep out of danger, and rode as fast as I could to tell you."

"That's right! Glad you did!" exclaimed Uncle Fred. "Now we must get to work right away to stop the fire from burning us out. Come on, boys!" he called. "Where's Captain Roy?"

"Here I am!" cried the former soldier, as he came out of the dining-room where he had been helping Margy and Mun Bun get up in their chairs, ready to eat. "What's the matter?"

"Prairie fire!" answered Uncle Fred. "We've got to stop it coming any farther this way, or it may burn all our ranch buildings down! No time for dinner now! We've got to fight the fire!"

"Can I help?" asked Russ eagerly.

"I want to just the same as him!" added Laddie.

Laura Lee Hope

"No, you boys must keep out of the way," answered Daddy Bunker. "I'll go and help Fred," he said to his wife. "You'll have to keep the children with you."

"I will," answered Mrs. Bunker.

"Oh, you don't need to do that," said Uncle Fred. "The fire is not near us yet, and if we can plow a wide strip of ground in time, the fire will come to the edge of that and stop. The older children can stand out of the way and watch the plowing, if they like."

"Can we see the fire, too?" asked Russ.

"Yes. Though you can't go very close," his uncle answered. "Let them have a look," he added to Daddy Bunker. "It isn't every day they see a prairie fire, and they'll never forget it. There will be no danger to them."

"All right," said Daddy Bunker. "Russ and Laddie and Violet and Rose may go to watch the plowing and see the fire. But Mun Bun and Margy must stay at home."

"I like to stay at home," said Margy. "I'm awful busy to-day."

"I like to stay at home, too," said Mun Bun, who generally did what his little sister did.

So with the two smallest Bunkers at home with their mother, the other four went with Daddy Bunker to see the fire and watch the cowboys at work.

When Uncle Fred had called the cowboys, they stopped whatever they were doing and began to get ready to fight the fire. Some of them had had their dinners, and others had not. But even those that had not eaten got ready to work. Captain

Roy hurried out, also ready to help.

"Get all the horses and plows you can find," said Uncle Fred. "If we haven't enough we'll borrow some from the neighbors."

Though no other ranchmen lived within several miles of Uncle Fred, still there were a few who had plows and horses that could be used. Uncle Fred had a telephone in his house, and Captain Roy was soon calling up the nearest ranchers, asking them to hurry with their plows and horses to make a big, wide strip of bare ground, so the fire would have nothing to burn.

"They'll be here as soon as they can," said the captain. "They have already seen the fire."

"I see it, too!" exclaimed Russ. "Look at the black smoke!"

"And I can see blazes, too!" exclaimed Laddie.

"So can I," added Rose.

"Who started the fire?" asked Violet.

"That we don't know," answered Uncle Fred. "Sometimes a cowboy may drop a match and forget about it. Again some one may start a campfire and forget to put it out when he leaves. All those things start prairie fires."

Uncle Fred and Captain Roy, and as many cowboys as could be found, started toward the cloud of black smoke with plows and horses. As Russ had said, the smoke-cloud could plainly be seen. It seemed to be rolling along the ground, as white, fleecy clouds roll along in the sky. And at the bottom of the black cloud could be seen fire.

The four little Bunkers were led by their father out to where they could have a good view of the fire. The smoke was blacker now, and the flames could be seen more plainly. At times, when the wind blew with unusual strength, the children could smell the smoke and burning grass.

"Does the wind push the fire on, same as it pushed Russ's sail-wagon?" asked Vi.

"Just the same," answered her father. "The fire comes toward us just as fast as the wind blows. If the wind would only blow the other way the fire would not harm us."

But the wind was blowing right toward Uncle Fred's ranch houses, and he and the cowboys knew they must hurry to plow the safety strip of land.

And so they began. Back and forth the teams of horses pulled the plows, turning the dry grass under and leaving only bare earth on top. Then other cowboys came, and the farmers and ranchers who had been telephoned to, and soon many were fighting the prairie fire.

Nearer and nearer it came. The horses, smelling the smoke and seeing the flames, began to snort and prance around.

"Only a little more now," cried Uncle Fred, "and we'll be safe!"

Back and forth the plows hurried, turning up strip after strip of damp ground. It was so hot now, because the fire was nearer, that Daddy Bunker led the children back a way.

"Could the fire get ahead of me if I ran fast?" asked Russ, as he watched the flames and smoke.

"Yes, if the wind blows hard the fire can go faster than the fastest man can run," said Captain Roy, who came up to where Daddy Bunker stood. The captain was thirsty, and wanted a drink of water from the pail Daddy Bunker had carried from the house.

"Do you think you can stop the fire?" asked Violet.

"Oh, yes, we'll stop it now all right," the former soldier answered. "We started to plow just in time."

And so it happened. The flames and smoke in the burning tall grass rolled right up to the edge of the plowed strip, and then they stopped. There was nothing more for the fire to "eat," as Russ called it. Some little tongues of fire tried to creep around the ends of the plowed strip, but the cowboys soon beat these out by throwing shovels full of dirt on them.

"There! Now the fire is out!" cried Uncle Fred. "There is no more danger."

"And will your houses be all right?" Rose asked.

"Yes, they won't burn now."

There was still much smoke in the air, but the wind was blowing it away. And then the children could see the big field, all burned black by the fire.

"The cows can't eat that now, can they?" asked Laddie.

"No, it's spoiled for pasture," said Uncle Fred. "But it will grow up again. Still a prairie fire is a bad thing."

The little Bunkers thought so, too, and they were glad when it was over. They went back to the house, leaving some of the cowboys on guard, to see that no stray sparks started another fire.

"And now we'll have dinner," said Uncle Fred. "It's a little late, but we'll call it dinner just the same."

He invited the men from the other ranches, who had come to help him fight the fire, to stay with him, and soon Bill Johnson was serving a meal to many hungry men. The little Bunkers had theirs separately.

That afternoon Russ and Laddie and Vi went fishing again, while Mrs. Bunker took the other children for a ride in one of Uncle Fred's wagons, with Daddy Bunker to drive. She went to call on a neighbor, about five miles away; a lady who used to live near Mrs. Bunker, but whom she had not seen for a long while.

Laddie, Russ and Violet had fun fishing, and caught enough for Bill Johnson to cook for supper.

"Come on!" called Laddie to Russ that evening, after they had played for a while out near the barn. "Let's go over and get a drink out of the spring."

"All right," agreed Russ. "Maybe we can see what makes it dry up."

"Maybe a bad Indian does it," suggested Laddie. "If I saw him do it I'd lasso him."

"So would I—only they won't let us have lassos any more."

"Well, maybe they would if they knew we could catch an Indian," went on Laddie hopefully. "Come on, anyhow." Then off they started toward the spring.

"Oh, look!" exclaimed Russ, who had run on ahead. "The water's all gone again!"

"It is?" cried Laddie. "Oh, we'd better go and tell Uncle Fred! Let me see!"

He hurried to his brother's side. Surely enough, there was hardly a pailful of water in the bottom of the spring. And the stream that trickled in through the rocks at the back had stopped.

"Do you s'pose the bad men are taking any more of Uncle Fred's cattle?" asked Laddie. "He said they did that when the spring went dry."

The two little boys managed to dip up a drink in the half a cocoanut shell, and then they looked about them. Night was coming on, and the sun had set some little time before.

"Hark! what's that?" asked Russ, listening.

"Thunder?" asked Laddie. "Is it thunder?"

"It sounds like it," said Russ, "but I don't see any lightning. I guess we'd better go home, anyhow."

They started away from the spring, and then Laddie suddenly cried:

"Oh, look! Look at Uncle Fred's cows all running away!"

Russ looked, and saw a big bunch of cattle rushing and thundering across the plain. It was the hoofs of the cattle beating on the ground that made the sound like thunder.

"Oh, what is it? What is it?" cried Laddie. "What makes 'em

run like that?"

"It's a cattle stampede!" shouted a voice, almost in the ears of the boys. "Look out! Up you come!"

# CHAPTER XVIII

## AN INDIAN

"It's a cattle stampede!"

Before Russ and Laddie had a chance to think what this meant, though Uncle Fred had told them in his stories, each little boy felt himself caught up in strong arms, and set on a horse in front of a cowboy.

What had happened was that two of Uncle Fred's cowboys had ridden along when Russ and Laddie were at the spring, and, fearing the little lads might get into danger, they had taken them up on their saddles.

"Where are we going?" asked Laddie, undecided whether or not to cry.

"We are going home—that is, I'm going to take you home," said the cowboy, smiling down at Laddie. "Then we'll try to stop these cattle from running away."

"Are the cattle running away?" asked Russ of the cowboy who held him so firmly in front on his saddle.

"That's what they are, little man," was the answer.

"Something frightened the steers, and they started to run. We've got to stop 'em, too!"

"Will they run far?" asked Russ.

"Well, sometimes they do and sometimes they don't," answered the cowboy. "It all depends. Out here on the plain, where there isn't any high land or cliffs for them to topple over, there isn't much danger. The cattle will run until they get tired out. But, of course, some of 'em get stepped on and hurt, and that's bad. And sometimes our cattle get mixed in with another herd, when they stampede this way, and it's hard to get 'em unmixed again. But we're going to take you two boys to the ranch house, and then we'll try to stop the stampede. What were you doing out here, anyhow?"

"Looking at the spring," answered Russ. "It's gone dry again."

"Has it?" asked the cowboy. "Then that means we'll lose more cattle, I reckon. Maybe the men started this stampede."

"No, I think this stampede was started by Indians," said the cowboy who had Laddie, and who had just ridden up alongside Russ in order to speak to "his cowboy" as Russ afterward called him.

"Indians!" cried Russ.

"Yes. Sometimes they come off the reservation, and start to travel to see some of their friends. A band of Indians will stampede a bunch of cattle as soon as anything else."

"Could we see the Indians?" asked Laddie.

"Well, maybe you can, if they come to the ranch. Some do to

get something to eat," was the answer. "But hold tight now, we've got to ride faster, if we want to get help in time to stop the runaway cattle."

So the two little boys held tightly to the horn, which is that part of the saddle which was directly in front of them. This horn is what the cowboys fasten their lassos around when they catch a wild steer or a pony.

Behind the boys could be heard the thunder of the hoofs of the stampeding steers. They were running close together, and, even in the half-darkness of the evening, a big cloud of dust raised by the many feet could be seen.

"What's the matter?" cried Uncle Fred, as the two cowboys rode up to the ranch with Laddie and Russ.

"Stampede!" was the answer. "Big bunch of cattle running away."

"Oh, my!" exclaimed Uncle Fred. "Well, get right after 'em! Stop 'em!"

And this is what the cowboys did. The two who had seen the stampede first, and ridden in to tell the news, bringing Laddie and Russ on the way, were joined by other cowboys. They then rode toward the rushing cattle, to head them off, or turn them back.

A stampede on a ranch means that a lot of steers or horses become so frightened over something that they all run together, and don't pay any attention to where they are going. If one of their number falls, the others trample right over it. So, too, if a cowboy on his horse got too close to the stampeding cattle, he would be trampled on.

To stop a stampede the cowboys try to turn the cattle around. This they do by riding along in front of them, as close as they dare, firing their big revolvers. They try to scare the steers from keeping on. Then if they can turn the front ones back, and get them to run in a circle—"milling," it is called—the others will do the same thing. The cattle stop running, quiet down and can be driven back where they came from.

It is hard work. Still it has to be done.

It soon grew so dark that the children and grown folk, watching from the house, could see nothing. Mrs. Bunker wanted the six little Bunkers to go to bed, but the four older children wanted to stay up and hear what the cowboys had to say when they came back.

"Well, you may stay half an hour," their father told them. "If they aren't back then off to bed you go!"

However, the cowboys came back about fifteen minutes later, saying they had stopped the stampede and turned the cattle back where they belonged.

"That's good," said Uncle Fred. "What with the fire and a stampede these are busy times at Three Star Ranch."

"And the spring is dried up again!" said Russ. "We forgot to tell you, Uncle Fred."

"The spring dried up once more? Well, I suppose that means more trouble and more cattle missing. I do wish I could find out this puzzle. Laddie, why can't you solve that riddle for me?"

"I don't know, Uncle Fred. I wish I could," said Laddie, as he was taken off to bed.

The next day Uncle Fred and Daddy Bunker went out to look at the spring, to take some more pictures of it with the camera, and see if they could find any reason for its going dry. Laddie and Russ and Vi, who usually wanted to go where her twin did, went with them, the other children staying at home to play.

"Yes, there's hardly any water in it," said Uncle Fred, as he looked down in the rocky basin at which Laddie and Russ had taken a drink the night before. "I think we'll have to dig back of those rocks," he said to Daddy Bunker, "and see what's behind them."

"It might be a good plan," agreed the children's father. "There may be some sort of secret channel through which the water runs out under the ground. I think I would dig, if I were you."

"I will," said Uncle Fred. "I'll go back to the house now and get picks and shovels. You can wait here for me."

"I'll come with you," said Daddy Bunker. "The children will be all right here."

"I'll go with you, Daddy," said Vi. "I must look after my mud pie I left in the sun to bake."

Uncle Fred started back toward the ranch buildings with Mr. Bunker and Vi, while Laddie and Russ sat down near the spring to wait. There was just a faint trickle of water coming through the rocks.

Suddenly the boys were surprised to hear a sort of grunt behind them, and, turning quickly, they saw a figure such as they had often seen in pictures.

"An Indian!" gasped Russ. "Oh, Laddie! It's an Indian!"

# CHAPTER XIX

## WHAT ROSE FOUND

There was no doubt about it. Standing in front of Laddie and Russ was an Indian. He was a tall man, with dark skin.

The Indian had a blanket wrapped around him, and on his feet were what seemed to be slippers, made of soft skin. Later the boys learned that these were moccasins.

In his hair the Indian had stuck two or three brightly-colored feathers. He was not a nice-looking man, but he smiled, in what he most likely meant to be a kind way, at the boys, and, pointing to the spring, said:

"Water? Indian get drink water?"

For a moment Russ or Laddie did not know what to think. The coming of an Indian was so sudden that it surprised them. They were all alone, too, for Uncle Fred and their father had gone back to the house to get shovels and picks to dig up the rocks back of the spring.

"Water? Indian get drink water?" asked the Redman again.

"Oh, he is a real Indian!" whispered Russ to his brother. "I see the feathers."

"Yes, and he's got a blanket on, same as the Indians have in the picture Mother showed us," added Laddie.

"Indian get drink!" went on the Redman, as he opened his blanket. The boys saw that he wore a pair of old and rather dirty trousers and a red shirt without a collar. Aside from the blanket and the feathers in his hair, he was not dressed much like an Indian, so the boys decided.

"There isn't much water here," said Russ, "but I guess you can get a drink. The spring has gone dry."

"Spring gone dry? That funny—plenty rain," said the Indian.

He stooped down and dipped the cocoanut shell in what little water was in the bottom of the spring.

However the Indian managed to get enough to drink, and then he seemed to feel better. He sat down on the ground near the two boys and pulled a package from inside his shirt. It was wrapped in paper and, opening it, the Indian took out some bread and what seemed to be pieces of dried meat. Then he began to eat, paying no attention to the boys.

Russ and Laddie watched the Indian with wide-open eyes. This was the first one they had ever seen outside of a circus or a Wild-West show, and he was not like the Indians there. They all wore gaily-colored suits, and had many more feathers on their heads than this man did. But that he was a real Indian, Russ and Laddie never doubted.

Having finished his meal, and taken another drink of water, the Indian looked at the boys again and said:

"You live here?" and he waved his hand in a circle.

"Not—not zactly," stammered Laddie.

"We're staying with our Uncle Fred at Three Star Ranch," said Russ.

"Oh, Three Star Ranch. Huh! Me know! Good place. Bill Johnson him cook!"

"That's right!" exclaimed Laddie. "He knows Uncle Fred's cook. He must be a good Indian, Russ."

"I guess he is. Maybe he wants to see Uncle Fred."

"Here they come back," remarked Laddie, and he pointed to his father and Uncle Fred, who could now be seen coming toward the spring, carrying picks and shovels over their shoulders.

"You got papoose your house?" asked the Indian, pointing in the direction of the ranch houses. "You got little papoose?"

"What's a papoose?" asked Russ.

Laddie didn't know, and the Indian was trying to explain what he meant when Uncle Fred came along.

"Hello! You boys have company, I see," said the ranchman. "Where did the Indian come from?" and he looked at the Redman, as Indians are sometimes called.

"He just walked here," explained Russ. "He was thirsty and he ate some bread he had in his shirt, and now he asked us if we had a papoose at our house."

"He means small children," said Uncle Fred. "Papoose is the Indian word for baby—that is, it is with some Indians. They don't all speak the same language.

"Where are you from, and what do you want?" Uncle Fred asked the Indian. "What's your name?"

"Me Red Feather," answered the Indian, at the same time touching a red feather in his black hair. "Me look for papoose. You got?"

"We haven't got any for you," said Uncle Fred with a laugh. "I guess none of the six little Bunkers would want to go to live with you, though you may be a good Indian. But where are you from, and what do you want?"

The Indian began to talk in his own language, but Uncle Fred shook his head.

"I don't know what you're saying," he said. "If you're lost, and hungry, go back there and they'll feed you."

"Bill Johnson?" asked the Indian.

"So you know my ranch cook, do you?" asked Uncle Fred quickly. "I suppose some one told you to ask for him. Well, he'll give you a meal, and maybe he can understand your talk. I can't. Go back there!" and he pointed to the ranch house.

The Indian got up, and as he walked away he was seen to limp.

"What's the matter? Hurt your foot?" asked Daddy Bunker.

"Much hurt—yes," was the answer, but the Indian did not

stop. He kept on his limping way to the ranch houses.

"Is it all right for him to wander around over your ranch this way?" asked Daddy Bunker of Uncle Fred. "Won't he take some of your horses or cattle?"

"Oh, no, the cowboys will be on the watch. I guess Red Feather is all right, though I never saw him before. The Indians often get tired of staying on the reservation and wander off. They go visiting. They stop here now and then, and Bill Johnson feeds 'em. He sort of likes the Indians. I suppose one he fed some time ago has told the others, so Bill has a good name among the Indians. Well, now we'll dig, and see what we can find out about this queer spring."

"Could we go to see the Indian eat?" asked Russ.

"I like him—he talks so funny," said Laddie. "Maybe he knows some new riddles."

"Maybe he does," laughed Daddy Bunker. "You can try him if you like. Yes, go along to the house, if you wish, and if Bill Johnson asks you why, say Uncle Fred sent Red Feather to be fed."

"Come on!" called Russ to Laddie. "We'll go back to the house and talk some more to the Indian."

Laddie and Russ reached the house just as Red Feather arrived, for he walked slowly.

"So you're hungry, eh?" asked Bill Johnson, when the Indian had spoken to him. "Well, I guess I can feed you. Where did you come from, and where are you going?"

The Indian waved his hand toward the west, as if to say he

Laura Lee Hope

had come from that direction, but where he was going he did not tell. Bill tried to talk to him in two or three different Indian dialects, but Red Feather shook his head.

He knew a little English, and his own talk, and that was all. But, every now and then, as he ate, he looked up at Laddie and Russ, who sat near, and said:

"You got more papoose?"

"I guess he wants to see the rest of you little Bunkers!" said Bill Johnson. "Maybe he heard there were several children here, and he wants to see all of you. Some Indians like children more than others. Yes, we have more papooses, Red Feather, though these are the biggest," and he pointed to Russ and Laddie.

"No got um so high?" asked the Indian, and he held his hand about a foot over the head of Russ. "Got papoose so big?"

"No, none of the six little Bunkers is as big as that," explained Bill Johnson. "Russ is the biggest. But what's the matter with your foot?" he asked Red Feather, for the Indian limped badly when he walked.

The Indian spoke something in his own language and pointed to his foot.

"It's swelled," said Bill. "Reckon you must have cut it on a stone. Well, you sit down in the shade, and when Hank Nelson comes in I'll have him look at it. Hank's a sort of doctor among the cowboys," Bill explained to Laddie and Russ.

While the Indian was resting in the shade, Laddie and Russ ran to tell their mother and the other little Bunkers about him.

"Is he a *real*, wild Indian?" asked Rose.

"He's *real*, but he isn't *wild*," Russ answered. "I like him. He likes children, too, 'cause he's always talking about a papoose. Papoose is Indian for baby," he told his sister.

The other little Bunkers gathered around Red Feather, as he sat outside the cook-house, and he smiled at the children. He seemed to want to tell them something as he looked eagerly at them, but all he could make them, or the men at the ranch, understand, was that he wanted to see a "papoose" who was larger than Russ.

"Maybe he wants a boy to go along with him and help him 'cause he's lame," suggested Laddie.

"No, it isn't that," said Uncle Fred, who, with Daddy Bunker, had come back from the spring. "He's worrying about something, but I can't make out what it is. Maybe some of the other cowboys can talk his language. We'll wait until they come in."

Hank Nelson, the cowboy who "doctored" the others, came riding in, and he agreed to look at the Indian's lame foot. Hank said it was badly cut, and he put some salve and a clean bandage on it, for which Red Feather seemed very grateful.

"No can walk good," he said, when his foot was wrapped up. "I go sleep out there!" and he pointed to the tall grass of the plain.

"Oh, no, I guess we can fix you up a place to sleep," said Uncle Fred kindly. "There are some bunks in the barn where the extra cowboys used to sleep. You can stay there until your foot gets well, and Bill Johnson can give you something

Laura Lee Hope

to eat now and then."

"Oh, I'll feed him all right," said the cook. "He seems like a good Indian. I wish I knew what he meant by that 'papoose' he's always talking about."

But Red Feather could not tell, though he tried hard, and none of the cowboys spoke his kind of language. So he went to sleep in the barn, on a pile of clean straw, and seemed very thankful to all who had helped him.

"Did you find out anything about the queer spring?" asked Mrs. Bunker of her husband and Uncle Fred that night, when the children had gone to bed.

"No, nothing. We dug up back of the rocks, but found nothing that would show where the water runs away to."

"And did you hear of any more of your cattle being taken away?" asked Captain Roy, who had been visiting his son at the nearest army post. This son was also Captain Robert Roy, for he was named Robert for his father, and was now a captain in the regular army. Captain Roy, the father, had just come back.

"Yes, a few were driven off, as almost always happens when the spring goes dry," said the ranchman in answer to Captain Roy's question. "It is a puzzle—beats Laddie's riddles all to pieces."

"I suppose he'll be getting up some new ones about the Indian to-morrow," said Captain Roy.

"If the Indian doesn't run off in the night with one of the ponies," said Daddy Bunker.

"Oh, he won't go," declared Uncle Fred. "He's being treated too nicely here. He'll stay until his foot gets better."

And, surely enough, Red Feather was on hand for his breakfast the next morning. The six little Bunkers ran out to see him. He looked eagerly and anxiously at them, as if seeking for the "papoose" who was a little larger than Russ.

It was that afternoon, when the children had been having fun playing different games around the house, corrals and barn, that Rose walked off by herself to gather some flowers for the table, as she often did.

"Don't go too far!" her mother called to her.

"I won't," Rose promised.

A little later Mrs. Bunker, who was washing Mun Bun and Margy, and putting clean clothes on them, heard Rose calling from the side porch.

"Oh, Mother! Come here! Look what I found!"

"What is it?" asked Mrs. Bunker. "I can't come now. Tell me what it is, Rose."

"It's the papoose Red Feather was looking for, I guess!" was the answer of Rose Bunker.

# CHAPTER XX

## LADDIE IS MISSING

Mrs. Bunker had Mun Bun in her lap, finishing the buttoning of his shoes, but, when Rose called out about the papoose, her mother quickly set the little fellow down on the floor, and ran to the window from where she could see her daughter on the porch.

"What did you say you had found, Rose?" she called.

"I don't know, for sure," said Rose, "but I guess it's the papoose Red Feather wants. Anyhow it's a little Indian girl, and she's bigger than Russ. Come on down!"

Mrs. Bunker hurried down to the porch, and there she saw Rose standing beside a little girl dressed in rather a ragged calico dress. The little girl was very dark, as though she had lived all her life out in the sun, getting tanned all the while, as the six little Bunkers were tanned at Cousin Tom's.

The little girl had long, straight hair, and it was very black, and, even without this, Mrs. Bunker would have known her to be an Indian.

"Where did you get her, Rose?" asked Mother Bunker.

"I found her out on the plain. She was lost, I guess. I told her to come along, 'cause we had an Indian man at Three Star Ranch. I don't guess she knew what I meant, but she came along with me, and here she is."

"Yes, so I see!" exclaimed the puzzled Mrs. Bunker. "Here she is! But what am I going to do with her?"

The Indian girl smiled, showing her white teeth.

"I'll tell Uncle Fred," said Rose.

"Yes, I guess that's what you'd better do," replied her mother. "Come up and sit down," she said to the Indian girl, but the little maiden Rose had found on the plain did not seem to understand. She looked at the chair which Mrs. Bunker pulled out from against the house, however, and then, with another shy smile, sat down in it.

"Poor thing," said Mrs. Bunker. "Maybe she belongs to Red Feather, and she may be lost. I wish she could talk to me, or that I could speak her language. I wonder—"

But just then Rose came hurrying back, not only with Uncle Fred, but with Daddy Bunker and Red Feather.

"What's all this I hear, about Rose going out in the fields and finding a lost papoose?" asked Uncle Fred.

"Well, here she is!" replied Mother Bunker.

Before any one else could say or do anything, Red Feather sprang forward, as well as he could on his lame foot, and, a moment later, had clasped the Indian girl in his arms. She clung to him, and they talked very fast in their own language.

Then Red Feather turned to Uncle Fred, and, motioning to Rose, said:

"She find lost papoose. Me glad!"

"So that's what he was trying to tell us!" exclaimed Uncle Fred. "Red Feather lost his little girl (his papoose as he calls her, though she isn't a baby), and he set out to find her. Then he hurt his foot and couldn't walk very well, so he came here. And that's what he meant when he tried to ask us if we had another—an Indian child—larger than Russ. This girl is bigger than Russ."

"Oh, I'm so glad she's found her father!" exclaimed Mrs. Bunker.

And that is just what the Indian girl had done. Later they heard the story, and it was just as Uncle Fred had said.

Red Feather and some other Indians, with their squaws, children, and little papooses, had left their reservation and started out to see some friends. On the way Sage Flower, which was the name of the Indian girl, became lost. She wandered away from the camp.

Her father and some of the other Indians started out after her, but did not find her. Then Red Feather, wandering about alone, hurt his foot, and managed to get to the spring when Laddie and Russ were waiting at it.

Red Feather tried to tell those at Three Star Ranch about his little lost girl, but could not make himself understood. Then his foot became so bad that he could not walk and he had to stay. And, all the while, he was wondering what had happened to Sage Flower.

The little Indian girl wandered about the plains, sleeping wherever she could find a little shelter, and eating some food she found at a place where some cowboys had been camping. They had gone off and left some bread and meat behind.

Poor little Sage Flower was very tired and hungry when Rose found her on the plain. The Indian girl did not know her father was at Three Star Ranch. She only knew she might get something to eat there and a place to sleep. So when Rose told her to come along Sage Flower was very glad to do so.

And oh! how glad and surprised she was when she found her own father there waiting for her. Sage Flower cried for joy. Mrs. Bunker then took care of her, seeing that she was washed and combed, and had something to eat.

The Indian girl could not speak her thanks in the language the six little Bunkers talked, but she looked her thanks from her eyes and in her smile.

A few days later Red Feather's foot was well enough to be used, and then he and his daughter were put in one of the ranch wagons and sent to the place where the other Indians were camping. The Redmen were very glad to see Red Feather and Sage Flower come back to them.

"Well, it's a good thing you found Sage Flower," said Daddy Bunker, "or the poor thing might have wandered on and on, and been lost for good. Her father, too, would have felt very bad."

But everything came out all right, you see, and Red Feather, to show how grateful he was to Rose, brought her, a week or so later, a beautiful basket, woven of sweet grass that smelled for a long time like the woods and fields.

With this Rose was immensely pleased.

There were many happy days at Three Star Ranch. The prairies did not get on fire again, and the cattle seemed to quiet down, and not want to stampede to make work for every one.

Russ and Laddie and Rose and Vi had fine fun riding their ponies to and fro, for they were allowed to go out alone, if they did not ride too far.

One day, after breakfast, Russ and Laddie came in to ask if they could go for a long ride all alone.

Rose was helping Bill Johnson in the kitchen, and Vi was busy lining a box in which to bury a dead bird she had found. Later there was to be a formal funeral with willow whistles for a band and as many people as would go in the funeral procession.

"I want to see if I can think of a riddle," said Laddie. "I haven't made up one for a long while."

"And I want to see if I can find that Indian, Red Feather," put in Russ. "Maybe he'll make me a bow and arrow."

"I'd rather you wouldn't go now," said their mother. "Don't you want to come with us?"

"Where are you going?" asked Laddie.

"Off to the woods for a little picnic. Bill Johnson is going to put us up a little lunch, and we will stay all day and have fun in the woods."

"Oh, yes, we'll go!" cried Russ. "We can ride our ponies

some other time," he added to his brother.

"All right," Laddie agreed. "Maybe I can think of a riddle in the woods."

"What makes them call it a 'woods,' Mother?" asked Vi later, when the lunch baskets were ready and the picnic party was about to set off. "Why don't they call it a 'trees' insteads of a woods? There's a lot of trees there."

"You may call it that, if you like," said Mother Bunker. "We'll go to the 'trees' and have some fun. Come on all my six little Bunkers!"

And away they went to the woods or the trees, whichever you like. There was a large clump of trees not far from the house on Three Star Ranch, and in that the children had their picnic. They played under the green boughs, had games of tag and ate their lunch. Then they rested and, after a while, Russ called:

"Come on! Let's have a game of hide-and-go-seek! I'll be it, and I'll blind and all the rest of you can hide."

"Oh, that'll be lots of fun!" said Rose.

So they played this game. Russ easily saw where Margy and Mun Bun hid themselves, behind bushes near the tree where he was "blinding," but he let them "in free." Then he caught Rose, and she had to be "it" the next time. Violet came in free, for she had picked out a good hiding-place.

"Now I have to find Laddie!" cried Russ. He hunted all over, but he could not find his little brother.

"Oh, tell him he can come in free!" exclaimed Rose. "Then

we can go on with the game."

So Russ called:

"Givie up! Givie up! Come on in free, Laddie!"

But Laddie did not come. Where could he be?

## CHAPTER XXI

## RUSS DIGS A HOLE

"What's the matter, children? Why are you shouting so?" asked Mrs. Bunker, who had walked on a little way through the woods to get some flowers. "Can't you play more quietly? You're as bad as the cowboys!"

"We're hollering for Laddie, Mother!" explained Russ. "We can't find him."

"Can't find him?"

"No. I was blinding, 'cause I was it, and he went off to hide. I found all the others, or they came in free, but I can't find Laddie, and he doesn't answer when I say I'll givie up."

"Perhaps he is hiding near here, and only laughing at you," said Mrs. Bunker. "We must take a look."

"Come on!" cried Russ to his brother and sisters. "We'll all look for Laddie. If he's doing this on purpose we won't let him play any more, either."

"Oh, I wouldn't say that," said Mrs. Bunker softly. "And, after all, maybe he went so far away that he can't hear you

Laura Lee Hope

telling him that he may come in free. So it wouldn't be fair not to let him play with you again. First find him, and then you can ask him why he hid away so long."

"All right, we will," agreed Russ.

So he and the others started through the woods, looking behind trees, under logs and back of bushes, hoping to catch sight of Laddie. But they did not see him.

Then they shouted and called.

"Givie up! Givie up!" echoed through the woods, that being the way to call when you want a person to come in from playing hide-and-go-seek. But Laddie did not answer.

"Where can he be, Mother?" asked Rose. "Is he hiding for fun, or is he lost?"

"I don't see how he can be lost, my dear," answered Mrs. Bunker. "He went to hide, and surely he wouldn't go very far away, because he would want a chance to run in free himself. No, I think Laddie must be doing a puzzle trick to make you find him. He probably is near by, but he is so well hidden that you can't find him. Try once more!"

So the children tried again, shouting and calling, but there was no Laddie.

"I think I'll go and get your father and Uncle Fred," Laddie's mother said to Rose and Russ. "They'll know how to find Laddie. You children stay here, and all keep together so none of you will be lost."

Mrs. Bunker did not have to go for help, for, just at that moment, her husband came up to them.

"Is anything the matter?" asked Daddy Bunker. "I was taking a walk over to the spring, to see if anything had happened to the water there, when I heard shouting and calling. Is anything wrong?"

"We can't find Laddie!" exclaimed Russ.

"He went to hide, but he won't come in," added Rose.

"I really am a little worried," said Mrs. Bunker. "Perhaps you had better get Fred and—"

"I'll find him!" said Daddy Bunker with a laugh. "He can't be far away. Show me where you blinded, Russ, when the others went to hide."

Russ showed his father where he had stood against a tree, hiding his head in his arms, so he would not see where the others were hiding. Standing at the same tree Mr. Bunker looked all around. Then he started off, walking this way and that, looking up and down and all around in the woods, until finally he stopped before a rather high stump, and said:

"Laddie is here!"

"Where?" cried some of the little Bunkers.

"I don't see him," said others.

"What's this?" asked Daddy Bunker, reaching up on the tree stump, and lifting down a cap.

"Why—why—that's Laddie's!" stammered Russ. "I saw it there before, but I thought he hung it there so it wouldn't fall off when he was playing."

Laura Lee Hope

"Well, we'll see what's inside this stump, for it is hollow," went on Mr. Bunker with a smile. "Unless I'm much mistaken we'll find in here—"

And just then, from inside the middle of the stump there stuck up a tousled head of hair, and Laddie's rather surprised face looked down at his father and mother and brothers and sisters.

"Oh, you found me!" he exclaimed. "I was going to run in free!"

"Why didn't you?" asked Russ. "I called 'givie up!' a lot of times."

"I—I didn't hear you," said Laddie, rubbing his eyes. "I guess I must have fallen asleep."

"That's what happened," said Daddy Bunker. "When I saw your cap hanging on a splinter outside the hollow stump I thought you must have hung it there while you climbed inside. Did you?"

"Yes," answered Laddie. "I was looking for a good place to hide, and when I climbed up on a stone, outside, and saw the stump was hollow I knew I could fool Russ. So I left my cap outside, and I got in. And it was so nice and soft there that I just snuggled down and—and I fell asleep. I was sleepy anyhow."

"Didn't you hear us calling?" asked Rose.

"Nope!"

"And didn't you hear me tell you to come in free?" Russ wanted to know.

"Nope. I guess I must have slept a lot," said Laddie.

"Well, I guess you did," agreed his mother. "We were alarmed about you. Don't do anything like that again."

Laddie promised that he wouldn't, and then he climbed out of the hollow stump. It was just high enough from the ground to prevent any one, passing along, from looking down into it. And Laddie could not have climbed up and gotten in if he had not used a stone to step on. The other children took a peep inside, Margy and Mun Bun having to be lifted up, of course.

The stump was partly filled with dried leaves, which made a soft bed on which Laddie had really gone to sleep. He had just curled up in a sort of nest and there he had stayed while the others were hunting for him.

"Are we going to play hide-and-go-seek any more?" asked Laddie, when he had climbed out of the stump and brushed the pieces of leaves off his clothes.

"I'm hungry," announced Mun Bun. "I want some bread and peaches."

"So do I!" added Margy.

Bill Johnson, the good-natured cook, did not have jam to give the children, as Grandmother Ford had done when they were at Great Hedge, so he gave them canned peaches instead. And they liked these almost as much.

"Well, I'll take Mun Bun and Margy to the house," said Mrs. Bunker. "You other children can play here in the woods, if you like. But don't any of you get lost again."

They promised that they would not, and, after Margy and Mun Bun had gone with their father and mother, Russ and Laddie, with Rose and Violet, played the hiding game some more.

But finally the two girls grew tired, and said they were going to play keep house with their dolls.

"Well, it's no fun for us two to play hide from each other," said Russ to Laddie. "What'll we do?"

"Let's guess riddles," suggested Laddie.

"No, that isn't any fun, either," said Russ. "You'd think of all the riddles and I'd have to think of all the answers. I know what let's do!"

"What?"

"Let's dig a hole."

"A hole? What for?"

"Oh, just for fun. Let's see how deep we can dig a hole."

"All right," agreed Laddie, after a while. "Maybe we can dig one deep enough for a well, and then Uncle Fred won't have to go to the creek after water when the spring goes dry. We'll dig a well!"

"We'll dig a hole, anyhow," said Russ. "Maybe there won't any water come in it and then it wouldn't be a well. But we'll dig a hole anyhow."

So Russ got some shovels at the barn, and he and Laddie began to dig a hole, starting it not far from the spring, though not close enough to get any dirt in the clear water that was so cool and sweet to drink.

Laura Lee Hope

# CHAPTER XXII

## AT THE BRIDGE

"Are you going to make a big hole so we both can get in at the same time?" asked Laddie of Russ, as the older boy began to shovel out the dirt.

"No, we'll take turns digging. If we made such a big hole it would take too long. First I'll dig and throw out the dirt, and you can throw it farther on, so it won't roll back in the hole. Then, when I get tired of digging in the hole, you can get in and dig."

"That'll be lots of fun!" exclaimed Laddie. "Won't Uncle Fred be s'prised when he sees a well full of water?"

"Maybe it won't be quite *full*," said Russ. "But we may get some."

The boys, of course, could not dig very fast. The shovels they had were rather small, and did not hold much dirt. But they were fully large enough for two such little boys.

The earth was somewhat sandy, and there were not many large stones on Uncle Fred's ranch. Of course, the digging was not as easy as it had been at the beach where Cousin

Tom lived, but Russ and Laddie did not mind this. They were digging for fun, as much as for anything else, and they really did not have to do it.

So they dug away, first one and then the other getting down in the hole, until they had made it so large that, even when Laddie stood up in it, his head hardly came up to the top of the ground. Russ, being taller, stuck a little more out of the hole than did his brother.

"Do you see any water yet?" asked Laddie, when Russ had been digging, in his turn, for some little time.

"No, not yet," was the answer. "It's awful dry."

"We could get some water from the spring and pour it in," said Laddie. "Then it would look like a well."

"But all the water would run out, if we just poured it in, same as it ran out when we dug a hole at the beach and let the waves fill it," objected Russ. "We'll dig down until we come to some regular water. Then it will be a real well."

But long before they reached water Laddie and Russ became tired of digging. They got to a place where the earth was packed hard, and it was not easy to shovel it out, and finally Russ said:

"Oh, I'm not going to make a well!"

"I'm not, either," declared Laddie. "What'll we do?"

"Let's go for a ride on our ponies," suggested Russ.

"All right!" agreed Laddie. "That'll be fun."

So, dropping the shovels at the side of the hole they had dug, instead of taking them back to the barn, as they should have done, Russ and Laddie went to the house to ask their father or mother if they might go for a ride on the little ponies.

Mr. Bunker was out on the ranch with Uncle Fred, but Mother Bunker said the two boys might ride over the plain if they did not go too far.

Russ and Laddie went to the corral to get their ponies. The boys got one of the cowboys, who was working around the barn, to put the saddles on for them, as this they could not do for themselves, and then they set off, Russ on "Star," as he called his pony, for it had a white star on its forehead, while Laddie rode "Stocking." His pony had been named that because one leg, about half-way up from the hoof, was white, just as if the little horse had on one white stocking.

"Gid-dap!" cried Russ to Star.

"Gid-dap!" called Laddie to Stocking.

And off and away, over the plain, the two ponies galloped.

"They sure are two nice little boys," said Bill Johnson to Mrs. Bunker, as they watched Laddie and Russ ride away.

"Yes, they try to be good, though they do get into mischief now and then," answered the little boys' mother.

On and on rode Laddie and Russ, their ponies trotting over the grassy plain. The day was warm and sunny, and the two boys were having a grand time.

"I wish I was an Indian," said Russ, with a sigh, as he let his pony walk a way, for it seemed tired.

"I'd rather be a cowboy," said Laddie.

"But Indians can live in a tent," went on Russ. "And if they don't like it in one place they can take their tent to another place. If you're a cowboy and live in a house, like Uncle Fred's, you have to stay where the house is."

"Yes," said Laddie, after thinking it over a bit. "You have to do that. I guess maybe I'll be an Indian, too."

"Let's both make believe we're Indians now," proposed Russ.

"We'll pretend we're out hunting buffaloes," agreed Laddie.

"And if we see any of Uncle Fred's cattle we'll make believe they are buffaloes and we'll lasso them," went on Russ.

"Yes, and we'll shoot 'em, too," declared Laddie.

"Only make believe, though!" exclaimed his brother. "I wouldn't want to shoot a cow really."

"No, I wouldn't either. But do Indians have guns, Russ?"

"Course they do. Didn't you hear Bill Johnson tell about how he saw a whole lot of Indians with guns?"

"Oh, yes. Then we'll be gun-Indians, and not the bow-and-arrow kind."

"Sure!" agreed Russ. "We'll get some sticks for guns."

They stopped on the edge of the woods to get sticks that would answer for guns. Then, after resting in the shade for a while, they rode on.

"Woo! Wah! Hoo!" suddenly yelled Russ.

"What's the matter?" asked Laddie, looking around at his brother, who was riding behind him. "What did you yell that way for?"

"'Cause I'm an Indian!" answered Russ. "You have to yell that way, too. Indians always yell."

"Oh, all right. I'll yell," said Laddie. "I thought maybe you'd hurt yourself. Oh, hoo! Doodle-doodle-oo!" he shouted.

"Hey, that's no way to yell like an Indian!" objected Russ.

"Why isn't it?"

"'Cause it sounds more like a rooster crowing. Yell like this: 'Wah-hoo! Zoo! Zoop! Wah! Wah!'"

"Oh, you want me to yell that way. Well, I will," said Laddie. And he yelled as nearly as he could like his brother.

So the two boys rode on and on, crossing the plain this way and that, so as not to get too far from the house. They could see the ranch buildings each time they got on top of the little knolls that were scattered here and there over the plain.

"Let's have a race!" suggested Laddie, after a bit. "I don't guess we are going to see any of Uncle Fred's cattle over here to make believe they're buffaloes. Let's have a race!"

"All right!" agreed Russ. "And I don't have to give you any head start this time, 'cause your pony's legs are going to run, and not your legs, and your pony's legs are every bit as long as my pony's. So we can start even."

"Yes," said Laddie, "we can start even."

They rode their ponies up alongside of each other, and got them in line. Then Russ said:

"We'll ride to the bridge. The first one there wins the race."

"Yes," said Laddie, "we'll race to the bridge."

This bridge was one across the creek, at a place where the water was deeper than anywhere else on Uncle Fred's ranch. The boys were told they must not cross the bridge unless some older person was with them, and they were not allowed to ride into the creek near the bridge because of the deep water.

"All ready?" asked Russ of his brother, as they sat on their ponies.

"All ready, yes."

"Then go!"

"Gid-dap!" cried Laddie.

"Gid-dap!" yelled Russ.

The ponies began to trot. Russ and Laddie did not have whips, and they would not have used them if they had had, for they loved their ponies and were very kind to them. But they tapped the ponies with their hands or their heels and shook the reins and called to them. This made the ponies run almost as fast as if they had been whipped, and was a great deal nicer. Besides, Russ and Laddie did not want to ride too fast, for they might have fallen off.

On and on they raced. Sometimes Russ was ahead, and again Laddie would be. But, just as they came near the bridge, the pony Russ was on slowed up a bit. Laddie's pony kept on, and so he won the race.

"But I don't care," said Russ kindly. "After we rest a bit at the bridge we'll have another race and I'll win that one."

"I hope you do, then we'll be even," said Laddie.

The little boys got off their ponies and looked about them. The ponies began to eat the green grass, and Laddie and Russ were looking for a shady place in which to cool off when they suddenly heard a groan. It was quite loud, and seemed to come from near the bridge. Then a voice called:

"Water! Oh, some one get me a drink of water!"

# CHAPTER XXIII

## THE BOYS' WELL

"Did you hear that?" asked Russ of Laddie, as they stared about them.

"Course I heard it."

"What did it sound like?"

"Like the ghost at Great Hedge," said Laddie.

"Yes," agreed Russ, "that's what it did sound like—a sort of groan. But there can't be any ghost here."

"Course not. But what was it?"

Laddie and Russ looked across the bridge, but could see no one on the other side.

Then the groan sounded again, quite near them, and the voice again called:

"Water! Water!"

"Somebody wants a drink," said Laddie.

"But who is it?" asked Russ. "I don't see anybody."

"It sounds like a man," replied Laddie.

"Maybe it's an Indian," said Russ. "But I don't guess Indians would talk as plain as that. Maybe it's one of Uncle Fred's cowboys, and he fell off his horse and is hurt."

"Oh, maybe 'tis!" exclaimed Laddie. "But if it's a strange cowboy we must ride right home. Mother said so."

"We got to get him a drink first," decided Russ. "You always have to do that. You have to do that even to an enemy, 'cause we learned that in Sunday-school. Let's see if we can find who 'tis wants a drink."

Suddenly the voice called again, so loudly and so close to them that Russ and Laddie both jumped when they heard it.

"Whoever you are, please get me some water!" said the voice. "I'm a cowboy and I've fallen off my horse and broken my leg."

"Where—where are you?" asked Russ, looking about.

"In the tall grass, right at the end of the bridge. I can see you boys, but you can't see me because I'm hidden in the grass. I was going to ride over the bridge, but my pony slipped and threw me and I've been here some time with a broken leg. Get me a drink if you can."

Russ and Laddie looked at each other. Then they looked toward the end of the bridge, where the voice sounded, and they saw the long grass moving.

"He must be in there," said Laddie, pointing.

"He is," answered Russ. "Here, you hold Star and I'll get him a drink," and Russ slipped off his pony, taking off the cap he wore. Russ had an idea he could carry some water to the cowboy in the cap, and in this he was right.

Going down to the edge of the creek, at one side of the bridge, Russ dented in the outside top of his cap, and filled it with water.

Then, carrying the cap as carefully as he could, Russ made his way to where the cowboy had called from. The little boy found the injured man lying in the tall grass.

"Ah! That's good!" exclaimed the cowboy, as he drank the water. "Now if you could catch my horse for me maybe I could get up on him, and ride him to where I belong. Do you see my horse anywhere?"

Russ looked all about. At first he saw nothing, but, as he gazed across the bridge he saw, on the other side of the creek, a big horse eating grass.

"I see him!" said Russ to the cowboy. "He's over the bridge."

"Is he? That's good. Then he didn't go very far away, after all. Now, look here, you seem to be a pretty smart boy," and the cowboy spoke in a stronger voice, now that he had had a drink of water. "Do you want to help me?"

"Yes," said Russ, "I'd like to help you. My mother says we must help everybody, and give them a drink of cold water, even our enemies, and I know you're not an enemy."

"I don't know about that," said the cowboy with a queer laugh, and he turned his head away and seemed to be looking at his horse, which was on the other side of the bridge, eating grass.

"No, you're not an enemy," went on Russ. "An enemy is a bad man, and you're not that."

"I wouldn't be so sure on that point, either," returned the cowboy. "But I won't hurt you, that's certain. Now look here, boy—"

"My name is Russ Bunker," interrupted the lad.

"Well, Russ, do you think you could go across the bridge and get my horse for me? If I had him I could ride away, now that I feel better after having had a drink. Will you cross the bridge and get my horse for me?"

"No," said Russ slowly, "I couldn't do that."

"Why not? The horse won't hurt you. He's so tame you could walk right up to him, and get hold of the reins. He won't run the way some horses do. You know something about horses or you wouldn't be riding one. Why won't you get mine?"

"'Cause Mother said I wasn't to cross the bridge alone," answered Russ. "Me or Laddie—we can't go across the bridge alone."

"Oh," said the cowboy. "But then your mother didn't know you were going to meet a sick man—one that couldn't walk. She'd let you cross the bridge if she was here."

"But she isn't here," said Russ. "I know what I can do, though! I can ride back and ask her if Laddie and I can go across the bridge for your horse. I'll do it!"

"No! Wait! Hold on a minute!" cried the cowboy. "I don't want you to do that. I don't want you to ride and tell any one I'm here. I'd rather you'd get my horse for me yourself. Just ride your horse across the bridge and get mine."

"I haven't a horse. I have one of Uncle Fred's ponies," said Russ. "And my brother Laddie's got a pony, too. But I can't go across the bridge. Mother said I wasn't to. But I'll ride to Three Star Ranch—"

"Are you from Three Star Ranch?" asked the cowboy quickly.

"Yes," answered Russ.

"Oh!" and the cowboy seemed much surprised. "Well, I guess I'd better get my own horse then," he said. "I guess no one from Three Star Ranch would want to help me if they knew what I'd done. Ride along, boy—Russ you said your name was, didn't you? Ride along, and I'll see if I can't crawl over and get my own horse."

Russ did not know what to do. He wanted to help the cowboy, who seemed in much pain, but the little boy was not going to cross the bridge when his mother had told him not to.

"Hey!" called Laddie. "Come on, Russ. I'm tired of holding your pony."

"All right," said Russ. "I'm coming. We have to ride back and ask Mother if we can cross the bridge to catch that horse!" and he pointed to the cowboy's animal, still cropping grass on the other side of the creek.

"No, don't bother about me," said the man in the grass. "I'll get my own horse. Always be a good boy and mind your mother. Then you won't get into trouble. I wish I had minded mine. Maybe I wouldn't be here now. Ride on home, but don't say anything about me."

Russ turned back to join Laddie. As he did so he saw the cowboy try to rise up and walk. But the man, as soon as he put one leg to the ground, uttered a loud cry and fell back. Then he lay very still and quiet.

"What's the matter with him?" asked Laddie, in a low voice.

"I don't know," answered Russ. "But I guess we'd better ride back and tell Daddy or Uncle Fred. They'll know what to do. We can't cross the bridge, but we can go for help. Come on!"

Russ got on his pony again, and he and Laddie rode away as fast as they could, leaving the cowboy very still and quiet, lying in the long grass at the end of the bridge.

Meanwhile something was going on back at the Three Star Ranch house. Uncle Fred and Daddy Bunker, who had been out riding on the plains, came galloping back.

"Where are Russ and Laddie?" asked their father of his wife.

"They went for a ride down by the creek," she answered. "They said they'd go only as far as the bridge. But they've been gone a long while, and I wish you'd ride after them and bring them back."

"I will," said Mr. Bunker. "Want to come for a ride, Rose?"

"Yes, Daddy."

"Well, I'll get your pony out of the corral, and saddle him for you. Then we'll ride and get Russ and Laddie."

A little later Rose and her father started out on their ride. As they passed near the queer spring, which, for the last day or so had not emptied itself of water, Daddy Bunker saw quite a hole in the ground.

"What's that?" he asked Rose.

"Oh, it's where Russ and Laddie started to make a well," she answered. "But I guess they didn't find any water."

Daddy Bunker got off his horse to take a look. He bent over the well the boys had dug, and stooped close down to it. As he did so a queer look came over his face.

"I wonder if this can be the place?" he said to himself.

"What is it?" asked Rose.

"I don't know," her father answered. "But it sounds to me like running water down near where Russ and Laddie have been digging. If it is, it may mean we can find out the secret of Uncle Fred's spring. I guess I'd better go and tell him. It won't take long, and then we can all ride on and get Russ and Laddie, if they aren't back by then.

"Yes, I shouldn't be surprised but what those two boys had started to solve the riddle of the spring. I must tell Uncle Fred!"

## CHAPTER XXIV

## MORE CATTLE GONE

Uncle Fred was out in the barn, talking over some ranch matters with Captain Roy, when Daddy Bunker and Rose came trotting back.

"What's the matter?" asked Uncle Fred. "Has Rose found some more Indian papooses?" and he laughed.

"Not this time," answered her father. "But those boys of mine, Fred, have dug quite a hole near your spring. I went past it just now, on my way to find Laddie and Russ. There is a queer sound of gurgling water seeming to come from the bottom of their 'well,' as they called it. They didn't strike water, but they came near to it. You'd better come and have a look."

"I will," said Uncle Fred. "Better come along, Captain Roy," he went on. "We may all get a good surprise. I'd be glad to have the secret of the spring discovered."

The three men and Rose rode back to the hole Laddie and Russ had dug. Then Daddy Bunker, Uncle Fred and Captain Roy got off their horses to listen more closely.

"Do you hear it?" asked Daddy Bunker of the children's uncle.

"I hear water running somewhere under ground," answered Uncle Fred.

"So do I," said Captain Roy. "I shouldn't be surprised if this was where the water either ran into or out of our spring."

"We must get shovels and dig," said Uncle Fred. "When we dug back of the rocks it wasn't in the right place, I guess. Laddie and Russ, by accident, have found the very place we were looking for. I'm sure it's a good thing I brought the six little Bunkers out to Three Star Ranch."

"Don't be too sure yet," laughed Daddy Bunker. "We haven't found the answer to the riddle, yet."

They were going to ride back to the barn, to get picks and shovels, when Mrs. Bunker came hurrying out to them.

"Oh, Fred!" she called to her brother. "Something has happened!"

"What?" he asked.

"Russ and Laddie—" went on Mrs. Bunker.

"Has anything happened to them?" cried Daddy Bunker quickly.

"No, they're all right. But they just rode up to the house greatly excited, and they tell a remarkable story about a cowboy with a broken leg, and say that he's lying in the grass at the end of the bridge. They're quite worked-up over it. Maybe you'd better go to see what it is."

"Yes," said Daddy Bunker, "I presume I had better hurry on to see about Russ and Laddie."

"The spring and the well will keep until you come back," observed Uncle Fred.

"We'll wait for you," added Captain Roy.

Mr. Bunker hurried back with his wife to the ranch house.

"Russ and Laddie are there," said Mother Bunker, and she told about the little lads having seen the cowboy, just as Russ and Laddie had told her. They had ridden home from the bridge, and reached the house just after Daddy Bunker and Rose had gone away.

"Well, boys, what's this I hear?" asked Daddy Bunker. "Did you really find a cowboy? Or was it an Indian?"

"Oh, it's a cowboy all right, and I got him a drink of water in my cap," replied Russ. "He wanted me to ride over the bridge to get his horse, but Mother said I wasn't to, and I didn't."

"That's a good boy," said his father.

"And the cowboy, I guess, is hurt bad," said Laddie. "He couldn't walk on one leg, and he shut his eyes and sounded like he was sick."

"Maybe he is, poor fellow," said Mr. Bunker. "We must see about him at once. I'll go for Uncle Fred," and he hurried back where he had left the ranchman and Captain Roy.

"A cowboy hurt!" exclaimed Uncle Fred. "Well, I don't believe it can be any of mine, or I'd have heard about it.

However, we'll ride over to the bridge and see about it. We'll see later about the noise of running water under the well that Laddie and Russ dug."

Rose wanted to ride with her father to the bridge, but he said as they might have to carry back the cowboy with his injured leg, she had better go to the house with her mother and the boys. So Rose did.

Together Uncle Fred, Daddy Bunker and Captain Roy rode to the bridge where Russ and Laddie had ended their race. They easily found the cowboy, who had fainted away when he tried to stand on his leg, which was broken. His eyes were open when the three men rode up, and he smiled, and seemed glad to see them.

"I guess I'm going to be laid up for a while," he said. "My pony threw me, and my leg doubled under me. I saw some boys, and tried to get them to go across the bridge for my horse, but they wouldn't—said their mother didn't allow them."

"That's right—they were my boys," said Daddy Bunker. "But now we'll take care of you."

"Where are you from—what ranch?" asked Uncle Fred, looking closely at the cowboy. "I never saw you around here before."

"No, I'm a stranger. I'm looking for work. But I guess I'll have to stay in bed a while now."

"We'll take care of you at Three Star Ranch," said Uncle Fred kindly. "We've got plenty of room."

It was no easy work to move a man with a broken leg from

the field near the bridge to the bunk-house of Three Star Ranch, but at last it was done, and then the doctor was sent for. He said the cowboy, who gave his name as Sam Thurston, would have to stay in bed for a while, until his leg got well.

Getting the cowboy to the bunk-house, and going for the doctor, who lived some miles away, took up so much time that it was dark before Uncle Fred, Daddy Bunker and Captain Roy had time to think about looking at the well Laddie and Russ had dug. And then it was too late.

"We'll look at it the first thing in the morning," said the ranchman.

"Didn't you want us to dig the well?" asked Russ.

"Oh, I don't mind," his uncle answered. "And maybe, by means of that well, we may find out the secret of the spring."

The six little Bunkers sat in the living-room, listening to Uncle Fred tell a story, just before they were sent to bed. This was one of their delights since coming to Three Star Ranch. Uncle Fred knew a lot of stories of the West—stories of Indians, cowboys, of wild animals, big storms, of fires, and of cattle running in a stampede.

Mun Bun and Margy fell asleep, one in their mother's lap and the other in Daddy Bunker's; but Rose and Vi, and Laddie and Russ stayed awake, listening to the stories told by Uncle Fred.

"I know a riddle about a bear," said Laddie, when his uncle had finished a story about one.

"A riddle about a bear?" exclaimed Mr. Bell. "Well, let's hear it, Laddie."

"This is it. Why does a bear climb a tree? Why does he?"

"Lots of reasons," answered Russ.

"Well, you have to give one to answer my riddle," said Laddie. "Why does a bear climb a tree?"

"To get the hunter that climbed the tree first," said Daddy Bunker.

"Nope!" laughed Laddie.

"To get out of the way of the hunter," said Russ.

"Nope!" and Laddie laughed again.

"Does he climb it to go to sleep?" asked Rose.

"How could a bear go to sleep in a tree?" Laddie wanted to know. "I'll tell you the answer, 'cause you can't guess. A bear climbs a tree when the dogs bark at him, so he can throw bark at the dogs. Isn't that a good riddle? You know trees have bark."

"But you didn't say anything about dogs and bark at first!" objected Vi. "If you had said about the dogs I could have guessed."

"Well, I wanted to make it hard," said Laddie. "Maybe to-morrow I'll think of another riddle without any dogs in it."

"Well, you four little Bunkers that are still awake had better go to bed so you'll be able to eat breakfast as well as guess riddles to-morrow," laughed Mother Bunker. "Come on! To bed with you! Mun Bun and Margy fell asleep long ago."

So off to bed they went, not even dreaming about the strange things that were to happen the next day.

About an hour after the six little Bunkers were in Slumberland, Captain Roy, who had been over to the bunk-house to talk with some of the cowboys, came hurrying in where Uncle Fred was.

"Anything the matter?" asked the ranchman.

"Yes," answered the captain. "More of our cattle have been taken!"

# CHAPTER XXV

## THE SECRET OF THE SPRING

"More cattle taken?" cried Uncle Fred. "When did that happen?"

"Just a little while ago," answered Captain Roy. "One of the cowboys just rode in with the news."

"Well, this is too bad!" cried Uncle Fred.

"I'll tell you what let's do," said Daddy Bunker. "It isn't very late yet. Let's go out and look at the spring."

"What for?" asked his wife.

"Well," answered the father of the six little Bunkers, "I want to see if the water has run out of it this time. Perhaps it hasn't, and, if so, it would mean that the taking away of Uncle Fred's cattle didn't have anything to do with the mysterious spring."

"Well, it will do no harm to take a look," said the ranchman. "Come along, Captain Roy. We'll see what it all means."

Taking lanterns with them, they went out in the dark night to look at the spring.

"It's just the same," called Daddy Bunker, when he had taken a look. "The water is almost out of it."

"Then we must start, the first thing in the morning, digging at the place where the boys made their well," declared Uncle Fred. "I must get at the bottom of the secret of my spring."

"And I'd like to find out who it is that's taking our cattle!" exclaimed Captain Roy. "I think, in the morning, I'll take some of the cowboys and have a big hunt. This business must stop. Pretty soon we won't have any ranch left at Three Star. I'm going to find the men that are taking the cattle!"

When the six little Bunkers awoke the next morning, there was so much going on at Three Star Ranch that they did not know what to make of it. Cowboys were riding to and fro, Uncle Fred and Daddy Bunker were dressed in old clothes, Captain Roy had a gun slung over his shoulder, and many horses were standing outside the corral, saddled and bridled.

"Are we going on a picnic?" asked Vi. "Is there going to be a parade? Is the circus coming? What makes so many horses? Is there going to be a prairie fire?"

"Well, I guess you've asked enough questions for a while, little girl!" laughed her mother. "Come and get your breakfast now."

"But what's going on?" insisted Violet.

"Two things," her father told her. "Your uncle and I are going to dig deeper in the well Russ and Laddie started, to see what makes the gurgling sound of water under the earth at the bottom of it. And Captain Roy is going to try to find the men who took Uncle Fred's cattle last night."

"Oh, can't we help?" asked Laddie.

"You may come and watch us dig your well deeper," his father told him. "But it would not be safe for little boys to go hunting men who take cattle."

Just as Captain Roy and a lot of cowboys were about to ride off over the plain and Daddy Bunker and Uncle Fred were going to dig at the boys' well, Mrs. Bunker came out of the bunk-house. She had gone to see if the man with the broken leg needed anything.

"He wants to see you," she said to Uncle Fred. "He says he can tell you a secret."

"Tell me a secret!" exclaimed the ranchman. "Does he mean about the mysterious spring, or the stolen cattle?"

"He didn't say," answered Mrs. Bunker. "But he wants you to come to see him."

So Uncle Fred went. He stayed a long while in the room where Sam Thurston, the strange cowboy, had been put to bed after his broken leg was set, and when Uncle Fred came out he was much excited.

"Wait a minute, Captain Roy!" he called to his partner. "I can tell you where to look for the cattle that were taken last night."

"Where?" asked the former army man, pausing at the head of his band of cowboys.

"Over in the gully by the creek. They're hidden there."

"Who told you so?"

"Thurston, the strange cowboy. And he has also told me the secret of the spring, so we won't have to do any digging, Daddy Bunker."

"We won't? Why not?" asked the children's father in surprise.

"Because the cowboy says the reason the water stops coming in at certain times is because of something that happens back in the hills, where my spring starts, in a brook that runs under ground after its first beginning. Back in the hills the men, who have been taking the cattle, turn the water into another stream. That's why it doesn't run into mine, and that's why my spring dries up."

"But why do the men shut off our spring water?" asked Captain Roy.

"They do it to make a wet place so they can drive my cattle across it, and no hoof marks are left to tell which way the animals have gone. Then, when the cattle are safely away, the waters are let run down where they always flow, and they come into my spring again. The taking of the cattle and the drying up of my spring are all done by the same band of men. That's why, whenever any cattle were taken, the spring dried up. One went with the other."

"How did Sam Thurston know all this?" asked Daddy Bunker.

"This cowboy with the broken leg used to be one of the band of men who took my cattle," went on Uncle Fred. "He just told me. He was on his way to see about taking more of my steers when his horse threw him at the bridge. That's why he didn't want to come to Three Star Ranch—because he had treated us so meanly.

"But when he saw how good we were to him he made up his mind not to be bad any more and to tell about the men. He knows where they hide the cattle after they steal them, and he says if we go there now we can get back the steers, and also catch the men who took them. And after this the spring won't go dry any more."

"Well, well!" exclaimed the children's father. "And to think that two of the six little Bunkers, by finding the cowboy with the broken leg, should help solve the spring mystery!"

"It is extraordinary!" exclaimed Uncle Fred. "But I knew as soon as I saw the little Bunkers in the attic that day I walked into your house, that they could do something. And they have. Now, Captain Roy, you and the cowboys ride on and see if you can get back our cattle."

Away rode Captain Roy and the cowboys, and some hours later they came back with the men, whom they had easily caught. They found the cattle hidden in a gully, or deep valley, near the creek, and the steers were driven back to their pasturage on Three Star Ranch.

Then the whole story came out. Sam Thurston and the others of the band, instead of raising cattle of their own, used to take those belonging to other ranchmen. They found it easy to take Uncle Fred's, and, by making a dam, or wall of earth, across the place where the stream started that fed his spring, they could turn it in another direction, making it flow over a path, or trail.

Along this trail, when the water covered it, the men drove the cattle they took from Uncle Fred's field, and the water covered, and washed away, any marks the cattle's feet made. So no one could see which way they had been driven.

When the stream was thus dammed it did not flow into the spring, which went dry. After the dam was taken away the spring filled again.

And so it went on. Each time cattle were taken the spring was made to go dry, and the men thus fooled Uncle Fred and his cowboys. The bad men would hide the cattle and sell them to other men who did not know they were stolen.

So the secret of the spring might never have been discovered except for Laddie and Russ making that race to the bridge where they found the cowboy with the broken leg.

Sam Thurston became good after that, his leg healed, and he worked for Uncle Fred for a number of years. The bad men were sent to prison for a long time, and had no more chance to take cattle from any one.

"But aren't you going to dig down in the well we made, and see what is at the bottom of it?" asked Russ of his father, a day or so after the cattle had been got back and the men sent away.

"Yes, I think we shall," said Uncle Fred. "I'd like to know what that gurgle of water is."

So they dug and found out. But it had nothing to do with the secret of the spring, after all. It was only an old pipe, that had been laid some years before by a man that had formerly owned the ranch, before Uncle Fred bought it. The man laid a pipe from the overflow of the spring to a chicken coop, so the hens could get a drink. Then the pipe became covered over, and the man did not think to tell Uncle Fred about it when the ranch was sold.

But the secret of the spring was found out, and never after that did it go dry, and no more of Uncle Fred's cattle were taken.

"So it's a good thing we came out to see you, isn't it, Uncle Fred?" asked Laddie.

"I should say it was!" laughed his uncle.

"I'm going to make a riddle about it!" went on Laddie. "I don't just know what it's going to be, or what the answer is. But it will be a riddle."

"All right," laughed Uncle Fred. "When you think of it tell me. And now have all the fun you can on Three Star Ranch. There are no more secrets to bother you."

"What makes 'em call it a ranch?" asked Violet. "Is it 'cause it has a branch of a tree on it? Or is it an Indian name? And where are all the Indians you said we'd see, Uncle Fred? And do the Indians and cowboys ever fight? And do the Indians have bows and arrows, and could I have a pony ride now?"

"Well, I'll answer the last question by saying you may," said Uncle Fred with a laugh. "As for the others, we'll see about them later."

"Come on!" cried Russ. "We'll all have pony rides!"

"And I'll get Bill Johnson to give us some cookies so we can play picnic!" added Laddie.

"Oh, wait for me," called Rose. "I must put my doll to bed before we start."

"I want to come!" shouted Mun Bun.

"Me, too!" added Margy.

"Bless their hearts! Let 'em have all the fun they can!" laughed Uncle Fred.

And that's just what we shall do with the six little Bunkers as we take leave of them, perhaps some time to meet them again.


THE END

# ABOUT THE AUTHOR

**Laura Lee Hope** is a pseudonym used by the Stratemeyer Syndicate for the Bobbsey Twins and several other series of children's novels. Actual writers taking up the pen of Laura Lee Hope include Howard and Lilian Garis, Elizabeth Ward, Harriet (Stratemeyer) Adams, and Nancy Axelrad.

# Choose from Thousands of 1stWorldLibrary Classics By

A. M. Barnard
Ada Leverson
Adolphus William Ward
Aesop
Agatha Christie
Alexander Aaronsohn
Alexander Kielland
Alexandre Dumas
Alfred Gatty
Alfred Ollivant
Alice Duer Miller
Alice Turner Curtis
Alice Dunbar
Allen Chapman
Alleyne Ireland
Ambrose Bierce
Amelia E. Barr
Amory H. Bradford
Andrew Lang
Andrew McFarland Davis
Andy Adams
Angela Brazil
Anna Alice Chapin
Anna Sewell
Annie Besant
Annie Hamilton Donnell
Annie Payson Call
Annie Roe Carr
Annonaymous
Anton Chekhov
Archibald Lee Fletcher
Arnold Bennett
Arthur C. Benson
Arthur Conan Doyle
Arthur M. Winfield
Arthur Ransome
Arthur Schnitzler
Arthur Train
Atticus
B.H. Baden-Powell
B. M. Bower
B. C. Chatterjee
Baroness Emmuska Orczy
Baroness Orczy
Basil King
Bayard Taylor
Ben Macomber
Bertha Muzzy Bower
Bjornstjerne Bjornson

Booth Tarkington
Boyd Cable
Bram Stoker
C. Collodi
C. E. Orr
C. M. Ingleby
Carolyn Wells
Catherine Parr Traill
Charles A. Eastman
Charles Amory Beach
Charles Dickens
Charles Dudley Warner
Charles Farrar Browne
Charles Ives
Charles Kingsley
Charles Klein
Charles Hanson Towne
Charles Lathrop Pack
Charles Romyn Dake
Charles Whibley
Charles Willing Beale
Charlotte M. Braeme
Charlotte M. Yonge
Charlotte Perkins Stetson
Clair W. Hayes
Clarence Day Jr.
Clarence E. Mulford
Clemence Housman
Confucius
Coningsby Dawson
Cornelis DeWitt Wilcox
Cyril Burleigh
D. H. Lawrence
Daniel Defoe
David Garnett
Dinah Craik
Don Carlos Janes
Donald Keyhoe
Dorothy Kilner
Dougan Clark
Douglas Fairbanks
E. Nesbit
E. P. Roe
E. Phillips Oppenheim
E. S. Brooks
Earl Barnes
Edgar Rice Burroughs
Edith Van Dyne
Edith Wharton

Edward Everett Hale
Edward J. O'Biren
Edward S. Ellis
Edwin L. Arnold
Eleanor Atkins
Eleanor Hallowell Abbott
Eliot Gregory
Elizabeth Gaskell
Elizabeth McCracken
Elizabeth Von Arnim
Ellem Key
Emerson Hough
Emilie F. Carlen
Emily Bronte
Emily Dickinson
Enid Bagnold
Enilor Macartney Lane
Erasmus W. Jones
Ernie Howard Pie
Ethel May Dell
Ethel Turner
Ethel Watts Mumford
Eugene Sue
Eugenie Foa
Eugene Wood
Eustace Hale Ball
Evelyn Everett-green
Everard Cotes
F. H. Cheley
F. J. Cross
F. Marion Crawford
Fannie E. Newberry
Federick Austin Ogg
Ferdinand Ossendowski
Fergus Hume
Florence A. Kilpatrick
Fremont B. Deering
Francis Bacon
Francis Darwin
Frances Hodgson Burnett
Frances Parkinson Keyes
Frank Gee Patchin
Frank Harris
Frank Jewett Mather
Frank L. Packard
Frank V. Webster
Frederic Stewart Isham
Frederick Trevor Hill
Frederick Winslow Taylor

Friedrich Kerst
Friedrich Nietzsche
Fyodor Dostoyevsky
G.A. Henty
G.K. Chesterton
Gabrielle E. Jackson
Garrett P. Serviss
Gaston Leroux
George A. Warren
George Ade
Geroge Bernard Shaw
George Cary Eggleston
George Durston
George Ebers
George Eliot
George Gissing
George MacDonald
George Meredith
George Orwell
George Sylvester Viereck
George Tucker
George W. Cable
George Wharton James
Gertrude Atherton
Gordon Casserly
Grace E. King
Grace Gallatin
Grace Greenwood
Grant Allen
Guillermo A. Sherwell
Gulielma Zollinger
Gustav Flaubert
H. A. Cody
H. B. Irving
H.C. Bailey
H. G. Wells
H. H. Munro
H. Irving Hancock
H. R. Naylor
H. Rider Haggard
H. W. C. Davis
Haldeman Julius
Hall Caine
Hamilton Wright Mabie
Hans Christian Andersen
Harold Avery
Harold McGrath
Harriet Beecher Stowe
Harry Castlemon
Harry Coghill
Harry Houidini

Hayden Carruth
Helent Hunt Jackson
Helen Nicolay
Hendrik Conscience
Hendy David Thoreau
Henri Barbusse
Henrik Ibsen
Henry Adams
Henry Ford
Henry Frost
Henry James
Henry Jones Ford
Henry Seton Merriman
Henry W Longfellow
Herbert A. Giles
Herbert Carter
Herbert N. Casson
Herman Hesse
Hildegard G. Frey
Homer
Honore De Balzac
Horace B. Day
Horace Walpole
Horatio Alger Jr.
Howard Pyle
Howard R. Garis
Hugh Lofting
Hugh Walpole
Humphry Ward
Ian Maclaren
Inez Haynes Gillmore
Irving Bacheller
Isabel Cecilia Williams
Isabel Hornibrook
Israel Abrahams
Ivan Turgenev
J.G.Austin
J. Henri Fabre
J. M. Barrie
J. M. Walsh
J. Macdonald Oxley
J. R. Miller
J. S. Fletcher
J. S. Knowles
J. Storer Clouston
J. W. Duffield
Jack London
Jacob Abbott
James Allen
James Andrews
James Baldwin

James Branch Cabell
James DeMille
James Joyce
James Lane Allen
James Lane Allen
James Oliver Curwood
James Oppenheim
James Otis
James R. Driscoll
Jane Abbott
Jane Austen
Jane L. Stewart
Janet Aldridge
Jens Peter Jacobsen
Jerome K. Jerome
Jessie Graham Flower
John Buchan
John Burroughs
John Cournos
John F. Kennedy
John Gay
John Glasworthy
John Habberton
John Joy Bell
John Kendrick Bangs
John Milton
John Philip Sousa
John Taintor Foote
Jonas Lauritz Idemil Lie
Jonathan Swift
Joseph A. Altsheler
Joseph Carey
Joseph Conrad
Joseph E. Badger Jr
Joseph Hergesheimer
Joseph Jacobs
Jules Vernes
Julian Hawthrone
Julie A Lippmann
Justin Huntly McCarthy
Kakuzo Okakura
Karle Wilson Baker
Kate Chopin
Kenneth Grahame
Kenneth McGaffey
Kate Langley Bosher
Kate Langley Bosher
Katherine Cecil Thurston
Katherine Stokes
L. A. Abbot
L. T. Meade

L. Frank Baum
Latta Griswold
Laura Dent Crane
Laura Lee Hope
Laurence Housman
Lawrence Beasley
Leo Tolstoy
Leonid Andreyev
Lewis Carroll
Lewis Sperry Chafer
Lilian Bell
Lloyd Osbourne
Louis Hughes
Louis Joseph Vance
Louis Tracy
Louisa May Alcott
Lucy Fitch Perkins
Lucy Maud Montgomery
Luther Benson
Lydia Miller Middleton
Lyndon Orr
M. Corvus
M. H. Adams
Margaret E. Sangster
Margret Howth
Margaret Vandercook
Margaret W. Hungerford
Margret Penrose
Maria Edgeworth
Maria Thompson Daviess
Mariano Azuela
Marion Polk Angellotti
Mark Overton
Mark Twain
Mary Austin
Mary Catherine Crowley
Mary Cole
Mary Hastings Bradley
Mary Roberts Rinehart
Mary Rowlandson
M. Wollstonecraft Shelley
Maud Lindsay
Max Beerbohm
Myra Kelly
Nathaniel Hawthrone
Nicolo Machiavelli
O. F. Walton
Oscar Wilde

Owen Johnson
P.G. Wodehouse
Paul and Mabel Thorne
Paul G. Tomlinson
Paul Severing
Percy Brebner
Percy Keese Fitzhugh
Peter B. Kyne
Plato
Quincy Allen
R. Derby Holmes
R. L. Stevenson
R. S. Ball
Rabindranath Tagore
Rahul Alvares
Ralph Bonehill
Ralph Henry Barbour
Ralph Victor
Ralph Waldo Emmerson
Rene Descartes
Ray Cummings
Rex Beach
Rex E. Beach
Richard Harding Davis
Richard Jefferies
Richard Le Gallienne
Robert Barr
Robert Frost
Robert Gordon Anderson
Robert L. Drake
Robert Lansing
Robert Lynd
Robert Michael Ballantyne
Robert W. Chambers
Rosa Nouchette Carey
Rudyard Kipling
Saint Augustine
Samuel B. Allison
Samuel Hopkins Adams
Sarah Bernhardt
Sarah C. Hallowell
Selma Lagerlof
Sherwood Anderson
Sigmund Freud
Standish O'Grady
Stanley Weyman
Stella Benson
Stella M. Francis

Stephen Crane
Stewart Edward White
Stijn Streuvels
Swami Abhedananda
Swami Parmananda
T. S. Ackland
T. S. Arthur
The Princess Der Ling
Thomas A. Janvier
Thomas A Kempis
Thomas Anderton
Thomas Bailey Aldrich
Thomas Bulfinch
Thomas De Quincey
Thomas Dixon
Thomas H. Huxley
Thomas Hardy
Thomas More
Thornton W. Burgess
U. S. Grant
Upton Sinclair
Valentine Williams
Various Authors
Vaughan Kester
Victor Appleton
Victor G. Durham
Victoria Cross
Virginia Woolf
Wadsworth Camp
Walter Camp
Walter Scott
Washington Irving
Wilbur Lawton
Wilkie Collins
Willa Cather
Willard F. Baker
William Dean Howells
William le Queux
W. Makepeace Thackeray
William W. Walter
William Shakespeare
Winston Churchill
Yei Theodora Ozaki
Yogi Ramacharaka
Young E. Allison
Zane Grey